PERIGORD

Text by Michèle Aué
        Julie Roux
with the assistance of
Brigitte and Gilles Delluc

Translated by
Simon Pleasance,
Gabrielle Silver,
and Barbara Jachowicz-Davoust

SUMMARY

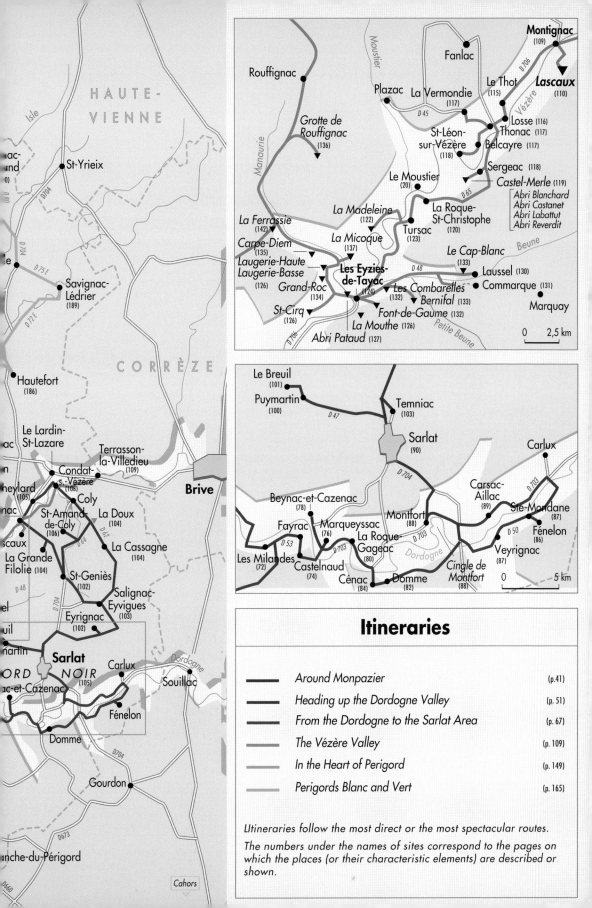

HAUTE-VIENNE

CORRÈZE

ORD NOIR

St-Yrieix

Savignac-Lédrier (189)

Hautefort (186)

Le Lardin-St-Lazare

Terrasson-la-Villedieu (109)

Brive

Condat-s-Vézère (108)

Coly

cheylard (105)

St-Amand-de-Coly (106)

La Doux

La Cassagne (104)

La Grande Filolie (104)

St-Geniès (102)

Salignac-Eyvigues (103)

Eyrignac (102)

Sarlat (105)

Carlux

Souillac

ac-et-Cazenac

Fénelon

Domme

Gourdon

nche-du-Périgord

Cahors

Rouffignac

Grotte de Rouffignac (136)

Fanlac

Plazac

La Vermondie (117)

Le Thot (115)

Montignac (109)

Lascaux (110)

Losse (116)

St-Léon-sur-Vézère (118)

Thonac (117)

Belcayre (117)

Sergeac (118)

Castel-Merle (119)

Le Moustier (20)

La Madeleine (122)

La Roque-St-Christophe (120)

Abri Blanchard
Abri Castanet
Abri Labattut
Abri Reverdit

La Ferrassie (142)

La Micoque (137)

Tursac (123)

Le Cap-Blanc (133)

Carpe-Diem (135)

Laugerie-Haute
Laugerie-Basse (126)

Les Eyzies-de-Tayac (124)

Laussel (130)

Commarque (131)

Grand-Roc (134)

Les Combarelles (132)

Bernifal (133)

Marquay

St-Cirq (126)

Font-de-Gaume (132)

La Mouthe (126)

Abri Pataud (127)

Beune

Petite Beune

0   2,5 km

Le Breuil (101)

Puymartin (100)

Temniac (103)

Sarlat (90)

Carlux

Carsac-Aillac (89)

Beynac-et-Cazenac (78)

Fayrac

Marqueyssac (76)

Montfort (88)

Ste-Mondane (87)

Fénelon (86)

Les Milandes (72)

Castelnaud (74)

La Roque-Gageac (80)

Veyrignac (87)

Cénac (84)

Domme (82)

Cingle de Montfort (88)

Dordogne

0   5 km

Itineraries

Around Monpazier (p.41)

Heading up the Dordogne Valley (p. 51)

From the Dordogne to the Sarlat Area (p. 67)

The Vézère Valley (p. 109)

In the Heart of Perigord (p. 149)

Perigords Blanc and Vert (p. 165)

LItineraries follow the most direct or the most spectacular routes.

The numbers under the names of sites correspond to the pages on which the places (or their characteristic elements) are described or shown.

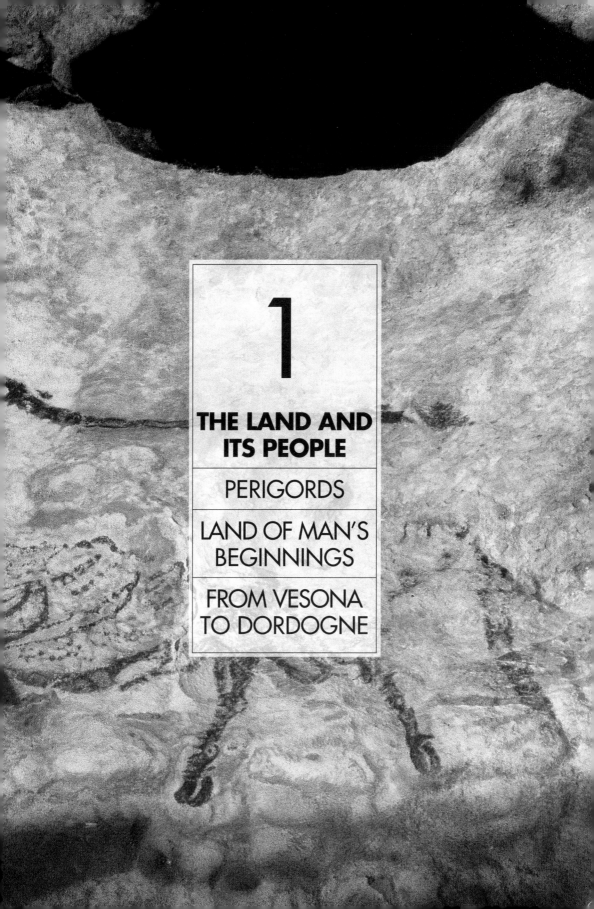

1

THE LAND AND ITS PEOPLE

PERIGORDS

LAND OF MAN'S BEGINNINGS

FROM VESONA TO DORDOGNE

1

PERIGORD, PERIGORDS

Perigord has been created by the human spirit. It is certainly not a uniform set of landscapes. Rather, it forms a patchwork of quite distinctive lesser regions, whence its special character, at once singular and plural.

In the singular, it closely matches the *département* of the Dordogne and nowadays, Perigord and Dordogne are often used interchangeably. Perigord is a borderline zone between the Massif Central to the east and the Aquitaine countryside to the west, the *causses* or limestone plateaus of Upper Quercy to the southeast and the ocean vistas of Charente to the northwest. During the Secondary Era (some 200 million years ago), the sea deposited these huge strata of Jurassic or Cretaceous sedimentary limestone on the ancient crystalline bed of the Massif Central. During the Tertiary Era the geological map was further complicated by the addition of large amounts of clayey sands from the Massif Central. Because of poor drainage, the Double and Landais regions developed forests, punctuated by ponds and pools large and small, like Lake Jemaye. Then, to the southwest, a small area of molasse – a mixture of lacustrine limestone, clay and quartz – much prized by wine growers in the Bergerac district was added. On top of all this, three deep parallel valleys run roughly east-to-west – the Dordogne-Vézère, the Isle and the Dronne. Their respective rivers either scour out deep beds, forming sheer cliffs, or casually spread their excess alluvial deposits, wrenched from hillsides, across the land. This region of hills, valleys, and narrow gorges offers a fine example of a complex landscape, difficult to illustrate by simple definitions or diagrams typical of geography books. There are no soaring mountains, no sweeping plains, no wide tablelands. Rather, it is as if nature has had fun blending several types of landscape to create a bucolic, pastoral region, on just the right scale for men and women.

These are gentle, entrancing landscapes, where the dark waters of rivers gleam, and perfect meanders are lined by the tremulous foliage of poplars. Forests combine with the wooded banks of smooth-flowing rivers and majestic rows of walnut trees to make Perigord a haven of wonderful, soft-edged freshness. And like a final brush-stroke to the picture, handsome and legendary castles – veritable complexes of towers, turrets, bartizans and pepper-pot pinnacles – loom around the next corner, their pale stonework trimmed by the even frieze of machicolations.

In the plural, Perigord becomes a patchwork of colours associated with this broad name, forming a somewhat artificial four-tone spectrum: white, black, green, and, just recently, crimson, for the Bergerac region. Yet its unity lies in the wealth of its gastronomy and the simple elegance of its traditional dwellings.

Black Perigord, with its prehistoric and historic troves, is the most celebrated. This vast, rolling limestone massif, never rising to more than 300 metres, is adorned, around Sarlat, with small conical peaks called *pechs*. The old districts of Sarlat, with their expertly dressed pale stonework, jealously guard their medieval spirit, and make this small town a historical centre of great importance.

The rivers Vézère and Dordogne converge at Limeuil, and conceal on their banks numerous prehistorical sites attesting to human activity dating back many millennia. Caverns and grottoes abound here, and offered a wide choice of overhangs providing shelter, and caves inhabited by people for many thou-

Perigord,
a Mouth-Watering Realm

The names of some regions release an aura of perfumes, and tastes, and powerful flavours. Perigord conjures up portly, plump geese, walnut trees laden with nuts, lush tobacco plants arrayed in neat rows, bashful truffles with their unique and subtle aromas, smooth wines from the hillsides of Bergerac and Monbazillac, the fragrant bolete or *cèpe*, and, most recent of all, the new Vergt strawberry. All this, and more, makes Perigord one of France's leading gastronomic heartlands. Within a matter of weeks, the tiny gosling with its incredibly soft down turns into the adult goose, a haughty, ill-tempered fowl, not the shy, waddling creature fondly depicted in popular imagery – behatted, basket on the arm, ponderous hindquarters swaying. Perigord geese are overfed, stuffed almost to choking-point with nourishing maize kernels, and nowadays esteemed solely on the basis of the probable weight of their liver. It is the firm consistency and slightly pale colour, and gently swelling contour of this organ that will decide whether it is a choice fattened *foie* or not. There is an extraordinarily unknown quantity about an equation otherwise thoroughly mastered, all the way from the moment of hatching to the final slice of the knife, revealing, within a splendid casket of golden fat, the prized liver, swollen and firm. Once cleaned, seasoned, and sealed with a fine sliver of truffle, it is then packed away in its humble tin can. You could not possibly guess what hidden treasure lies inside, were it not for the label proudly proclaiming a *foie gras* in finest lettering. But Perigord has another more particular star, one that people quest after, swear they have seen, and forever hope to find. A star that is becoming ever rarer: the truffle. Truffles are black, roundish, light, firm and, above all, enveloped, like some gift from the gods, in an inimitable perfume, at once penetrating and delicate. These fungi, buried in the warm

Vergt strawberries

Goose Farm

latest arrival, now swiftly colonizing the recently cleared woodland of the Vergt and Rouffignac region is the cultivated strawberry, which has retained the slightly acidulous flavour of its little sister, the wild strawberry. In the tumbling rivers of Perigord, trout, salmon and eels offer fugitive glimpses of their presence. Prepared with time-honoured recipes, they are a faithful feature of the sumptuous menus in these parts.Perigord is also wine country. Bergerac wines have effortlessly met the high standards of quality demanded of any great French *appellation d'origine contrôlée* – guaranteed vintage – wine. Be it red, white or rosé, Bergerac is for drinking young. "Côtes de Bergerac" wines differ widely in character, from colour to colour. The reds are robust, the whites mellow. Pécharmant is a good red wine for laying down, while Montravel is a sweet or dry white. Saussignac and Rosette wines are mellow whites, produced only in small quantities.

loam beneath oak forests, do not announce themselves by princely raiment. To detect these "black diamonds", you must decipher the very texture of the undergrowth, with its thousand-and-one cryptic, but revealing, details. Truffle-gathering is the preserve of the true connoisseur, and all to the good, for this helps protect truffles, and safeguard them from overly intensive exploitation. Their worth is now based on their rarity value, and truffle prices reach dizzy heights. But then, who would dream of applying real weights and measures to such fragrance? With its handsome, upright trunk, its even, open branches, and its long, soft green leaves, the walnut is the quintessential tree. In their orderly rows, walnut trees form the rustling backdrop of Perigord. In their stubborn shells, the nuts offer a savoury taste of still warm autumn days. The walnut may look deceptively like a dry fruit, but it also provides us with oils and liqueurs. The

Truffles

sands of years before their descendants built their fortresses on the cliffs above. The face of the rock-wall is flecked with a host of round, gaping holes, evidence of the remnants of troglodytic dwellings from the Middle Ages. The rivers brought to these parts not only innovation, wealth and progress, but, for many a century, danger too. Their trade routes gave birth to generations of skilled, brave bargemen who possessed the art of "listening to the river's moods". The rich Perigord oak forests supplied the raw material essential to the vast, rich vineyards of Bergerac and its environs. While the chestnut woodlands on the hills around Sarlat (called the Sarladais), the forests of Barade, haunted by Jacquou le Croquant, and La Bessède around Cadouin, all have a rich undergrowth of delicate ferns hiding fragrant chanterelle and boletus mushrooms – *cèpes*. The name Bergeracois or Crimson Perigord conjures up a flood of jostling images which eventually form a whole picture. Bergerac equals Cyrano. Needless to say, Cyrano was not from these parts, but he has been happily adopted by this small town. Bergerac equals wine, too – a famous hillside wine with evocative names like Pécharmant, Rosette, Montravel and, best known of all perhaps, Monbazillac, a vintage just sweet and golden enough. Bergerac also equals tobacco, here called *tabak*, of a brown and distinctly scented variety. The Double and Landais regions, lying north and south of the river Isle in the westernmost part of the *département*, boast extensive forests, too. The sandy, clayey soil here is poorly drained, so retains all the water that cannot be carried off by the countless streams, forming shallow expanses of surface water and deep pools alike, adorned with reeds and porcelaine-like water-lilies. Chestnut and hornbeam copses mingle with the delicate foliage of oak and maritime pine. This latter species, thriving on a soil that suits it to a tee, is the most recent arrival, with plantations dating back no fur-

Navigation on the Dordogne River

B ecause of its river network, Perigord was able to compensate for its lack of roads. Up until the 19th century, the Dordogne River played an essential role in the local economy. For regional products, wines from Bergerac, for example, or juniper wood or berries, it offered an opening into the Aquitaine market while allowing the importation of foodstuffs from the ocean: salt, dried or salted fish, along with sugar and products manufactured in Bordeaux. Ports or *peyrats*, simple outfitted embankments, were bustling with the crowds of people whose livelihood depended on the waters of the Dordogne: fishermen, ferrymen, haulers, dockers or merchants and the bargemen, of course. Rapids, loops, the narrowing of the riverbed and other meteorological hazards awaited these men but they let their experience guide them. The departure-time was always carefully chosen, when at the end of the summer the waters became "trade routes", that is to say, navigable. From Argentat all the way to Bergerac, the transport of goods was carried out on locally made flatbottom boats called *argentats*. Too fragile to make the return trip upriver, they were sold as planks or used for local trade once they had arrived at their destination. *Gabares* or *couraux*, long boats which could transport up to fifty barrels, took over from there to Libourne where the seagoing ships and riverboats met. When it came time for the river's ascent, and when the tide's effects would weaken past Castillon, men and oxen took over to tow the gabares to their home port in Bergerac. In the 19th century, this river traffic accounted for 50.000 tonnes of merchandise before competition with the railroad brought it to an end.

A thousand and one castles

From time immemorial, Perigord has been the land of a thousand and one castles. God, indeed, must have stopped to empty his castle-laden pockets just over Perigord. Unfortunately, war and insecurity were more often the inspiration for fortresses on this territory, long vulnerable to invasion through its river network and situated right on the border of English and French lands. Moreover, there were a great number of aristocrats in Perigord. As early as the 10th century, the bishop Frotaire had five forts built along the different rivers. During the Middle Ages, fortified towns grew in number, making good use of the geography of the region; hills and small valleys provided unobstructed views, steep cliffs were difficult to attain

Vestiges of Fages Castle from the 15th and 16th centuries

Campagne Castle

and strategic positions controlled points of passage. From the Roman keep to the Gothic fortress, the castle evolved along with progress in techniques of siege. During the 16th century, when the wars in Italy brought both new wealth and the taste for things Italian, the great lords of Perigord, at the height of their prestige, had grand residences built for themselves in the Renaissance style. After the Wars of Religion, while peace gradually settled in, the fortress took on a softer appearance. Transformed according to the fashion, the old fortified castles were decorated with paintings and sculptures and opened themselves to the landscape with pleasure. From then on, buildings were no longer maintained by wars but rather by farming and agriculture, particularly wine-growing. Beginning in the 17th century, the countryside was covered with prosperous single-storey, rural dwellings. In the 19th century, notables and bourgeois made a return to the land, launching a last wave of construction before new squires, industrialists and stars arrived to bring the thousand and one castles of Perigord back to life.

ther than the 19th century. In the very north of the *département*, the Nontronnais or Green Perigord region is essentially a huge glacis or incline of crystalline rocks, with deep gashes hewn by torrents spilling from the water tower formed by the nearby Massif Central. Tumbling streams and small rivers such as the Bandiat, Dronne, Côle, Isle, Loue and Auvézère still wind their arduous way through narrow passages like the Auvézère Gorge downstream from Savignac-Lédrier. South of Ribérac, the vegetation gradually thins until the landscape is a totally different one. White Perigord seems like a vast clearing in a *département* where the tree is king. The river Dronne forms a comely, tranquil valley, lined first with rocks, and then with gentle terracing, enhanced by rows of thrusting poplars. The hillsides drained by the middle reaches of the Isle valley form Central Perigord. Here, at the heart of this palette of bright-coloured Perigords, there is no single dominant hue. No one dominant colour maybe, but the same cannot be said of the region's well-tempered soul! The town of Périgueux is the region's heart – and jewel. Back in Gallo-Roman times, when it was an important town called Vesona. In the Middle Ages, it was a stage on the road to Santiago de Compostela with its cathedral of Saint Etienne-de-la-Cité, and then Saint Front Cathedral. Périgueux emerged emaciated from the bloody Hundred Years War. But in the early 16th century the town stirred anew. The Renaissance saw the construction of the handsome residences that grace the old central parts of the town, despite the ravages of the Wars of Religion. In the 18th century, the administrator Tourny was the driving force behind a major programme of urban replanning. In 1793, the town was chosen as the administrative seat of the *département* of the Dordogne. So Périgueux is twofold: capital of a small area that gave birth to European man, and heart of a modern region with an impressive array of attractions for the visitor.

The Knives of Nontron

Nontron was already making its knives in the 15th century when, with their solid steel blades crafted by the forges along the Bandiat riverbank, they carried the town's name well beyond the borders of Perigord. Knives for commoners and for aristocrats, they were also used by Parisian thugs, the *apaches,* and during World War I Nontron manufactured a tool for the "trench cleaners". Turned out of regional boxwood, the handles take on varied shapes: ball, clog, violin, or carp's tail. Their signature colour, a honeyed hue, is only truly attained when time has given them their proper patina. Steel blades, brass ferrules, golden handles, these are the principal characteristics of the large kitchen knife's ancestor. But since the end of the 19th century, Nontron also has its very own signature. From the table knife to the miniature knife, all of today's production is accented with a logo burned into the wood by pyrography: an upsidedown "V" marked with three dots. Every summer, knife lovers come from all over to assemble at a festival dedicated to the knife and its craft.

Nontron Knife

The Perigord-Limousin Regional Natural Park

Listed in 1998, the Perigord-Limousin Regional Natural Park groups together the northern cantons of the Dordogne and the south of the department of Haute-Vienne, seventy-eight communes in all. Situated in a contact zone between the Aquitaine basin and the Massif Central, four territories follow each other in distinct geographic zones: the Limousin bocage and its rolling plateau to the north; the massif des Feuillardiers at the park's centre, covered in wooded hills where the chesnut tree is king; the plateaux des Jumilhacois to the east of the Dronne River, carved out with narrow valleys where iron and gold were mined for a long time; and finally, to the southwest of the park, the open Perigourdian valleys, with the centre situated along the Nizonne River, between Mareuil and Nontron. Sparsely populated, with an average of 28 inhabitants per square kilometre, this territory gains an undeniable richness from the great diversity of its natural environment. The protection and promotion of this environment are the park's major focus. Thousands of species of flora and fauna can be found in various habitats. There are mammals such as the genet, birds such as the species of short-toed eagle called Jean le Blanc, insects, amphibians, reptiles and flowers such as the orchid, to name a few. To protect this natural environment, the entire landscape is taken into account, integrating both stream and field, or castle and church without forgetting the more secular architecture, the forges, mills and the chesnut driers which are a testimony to the local economy where water and wood played a major role. But there is also the heritage of folk traditions and the still living *savoir-faire* of artisans such as *la fête des soufflets*, the Bellows fair, and knife manufacturing in Nontron.

Chestnut-husk

The Chalard waterfall, in the heart of the Perigord-Limousin Regional Natural Park

The traditional Perigord dwelling

As in many of France's provinces, the traditional Perigord dwelling blends perfectly with the natural landscape. For raw materials, it draws on the rich resources of the land and what lies beneath it. These robust Perigord houses are built to a simple, square design. The tall, pale limestone walls are pierced by small windows with thick shutters. The striking, dark-tiled roofs are often steeply pitched, their timbers designed to bear the colossal weight of the overlapping roofing slabs, called *lauzes*. With an average load of a good 60-70 lbs. per square foot, these roofs seem to defy the very laws of gravity. The steep angle of the frame transfers the bulk of the weight on to the walls, thus achieving a more balanced distribution of the overall load. With half-timbered cob or daub façades, scattered traditional homes in the Double forest are

Dovecote

Lauze-covered roof

Le Breuil huts, near
Saint-André-d'Allas

...ow all that remain of a once very
...idespread style of rural architecture.
...ovecotes are two-a-penny, each one with
...s own special character. Built for the
...ost part during the 18th century, they
...ten tell a tale of noble privilege – a tax
...ayable by the peasantry based on the
...ize of the structure. Pigeons were kept in
...articular for their droppings or guano,
...ocally called *colombine,* and used as
...n excellent fertilizer well before the days
...f the chemical industry. These dovecotes
...re nearly always raised off the ground,
...uilt on solid pillars with a salient
...apstone cunningly laid to stop all manner
...f predator from gaining access.But there
...re still skillfully restored old dwellings
...n display in Perigord, at the André
...oulgre Museum of Popular Arts and
...rafts in Mussidan, for example, where
...isplays of furniture, tools, household
...bjects and farm machinery all conjure up
... style of life that is a little antiquated, but
...ill thoroughly captivating.

Half-timbered houses,
Myrpe Square,
Bergerac

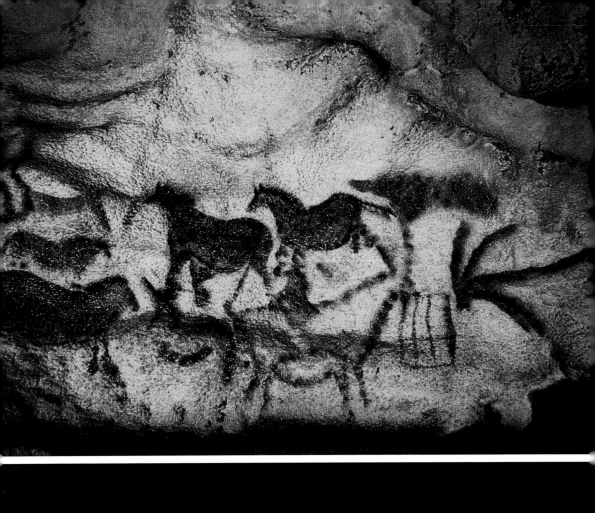

2

LAND OF MAN'S BEGINNINGS

Where prehistory is concerned, the Dordogne valley and, even more so, the Vézère valley, with such exceptional sites as Lascaux, La Micoque, Le Moustier and La Madeleine, are in a class of their own. These two valleys contain outstanding treasures, with well over a hundred prehistoric sites in the vicinity of Les Eyzies, with over two hundred in the Dordogne department.

Evidence abounds from the Paleolithic era (the "early" (chipped) Stone Age) to the Neolithic ("late" (polished) Stone Age), offering keen-eyed visitors a thrilling outline of the infinitely gradual but relentless evolution of the human species. And still the presence of man in the Dordogne does not date back any further than 350.000 years (B.P. - Before Present).

So we are at a considerable remove from the earliest *Hominidae* and other species of *Australopithecus*, all of whom were forced to adapt, almost three million years ago, to the tectonic and climatic upheavals occurring in East Africa.

The Great Rift Valley in Africa has transformed both landscape and climate at a stubborn, almost furtive snail's pace. West Africa, with plentiful rain and a lush carpet of forest, contrasted sharply with the drier east, where forests shrank and the savannah gained ground. The shelter afforded by the western forests helped to establish the evolution of a line culminating in our present-day gorillas and chimpanzees.

To the east, the dangers inherent in more open and sparsely wooded surroundings called for adaptations in some of its inhabitants. A hesitant upright posture, better adapted teeth, an enlarged more rounded skull, and, most important of all, the vital need to extend the scope of the hand with objects swiftly developing into proper tools all make *Australopithecus* into pre-humans 6 million years ago, no longer exactly an ape, but not quite modern man either. The symbol of this evolutionary phase is Lucy, unearthed in 1974 at Afar in Ethiopia. A piece of jaw from an *Australopithecus* named Abel was recently found in Chad.

Then a new arrival asserted himself 2.5 million years ago. This earliest man was better adapted to the climatic variations slowly altering the natural habitat. Even more significantly, he could make tools. The steady disappearance of forest, replaced by open, grassy spaces, created *Homo habilis*, with a more developed brain and teeth suited to an omnivorous diet. The final millennia of *Australopithecus* were thus spent alongside a less fussy, or perhaps greedier, *Homo habilis*, broadening his choice of food. Meat means game, which means hunting. *Homo habilis* was inventive and inquisitive, and equipped himself with even surer means of survival – mastering the upright position and tools fashioned from broken pebbles.

Homo erectus, standing upright, appeared in Africa 1.7 million years ago. His skull was still somewhat flat, but more spacious (900-1200 cc), with the forehead receding over beetling brows, the face prognathous but still chinless – a clear reminder of his distant simian origins. *Homo erectus* cropped up in Asia and Europe. He is, of course, still evolving. He is our direct ancestor, and some people like him lived at Caume de l'Arago near. Tautavel (just north of Perpignan), 450.000 years ago! *Homo erectus* was both observant and crafty. Early on, he acquired that commodity that is so colourful, bright, hot, and terrifyingly dangerous – something he would first gropingly learn to master, then actually make. After tools, man's unparalleled discovery is fire. His diet changed. He no longer felt the cold so much, for he could now huddle over a hearth. And this in turn produced group living. He started to construct a social order with carefully thought-out rules and customs. His shelter was now a hut made of branches, often snugly situated at the foot of cliffs, concealing long, murky fissures which he hesitated to explore because they housed wild animals. Instead, he had to make do with natural rock shelters beneath overhanging crags. Over thousands of years, he learned how to turn these stones so crucial to him – hard pebbles of quartz and nuggets of flint – into a single type of implement: biface, flat, oval, and edged, well-suited to every need, for it could cut, pierce, scratch, scrape, stun and kill!

The climate slowly changed, with periods of glaciation alternating with warmer times. The slow itinerary of *Homo erectus* took him eventually to Perigord, where the oldest

Le Moustier

Opposite the cliff face of La Roque-Saint-Christophe, once seething with the life of people occupying its troglodytic shelters, the small village of Le Moustier has lent its name to an important moment in the long Paleolithic period – the Mousterian age. This prehistoric site has yielded the skeleton of a Neanderthal man. A study of the series of settlements within this deposit, as well as of the flint tools it concealed, has helped to define the stages of the Mousterian period. The typical tools of those remote times, carved out of flint, are fairly small bifaces, with pointed tips, and scrapers with sharped edges. These tools were wielded by people living in the Middle Paleolithic period, some 100.000 to 35.000 years ago, during the Würm glaciation.

The Moustier Shelter

Archaeological excavations

In the realm of prehistory, excavations are essential, but they also pose a terrible dilemma, because the archaeologist is at once destroying the object of his quest as well as advancing his investigations. You can only dig up the same spot once! The objects unearthed are preserved, but never again in conjunction with their surrounding substrate. This painstaking task calls not for pick and shovel, but for pen-knives, scrapers, and brushes large and small. Nothing must be dislodged or broken. The archaeologist's top priority is to make a meticulous record of every aspect of the site, while at the same keeping part of the deposit intact for subsequent inspection. By using *stratigraphy*, it is possible to record the position of an object on both the vertical and horizontal plane. *Palaeontology*, the study of fossilized bodies, helps to establish chronological classifications based on an analysis of bones found in situ. *Palynology* is the study of fossilized pollen contained in different soils, and with *dendrochronology* it is possible to date fossil trees by indexing each of the concentric annual growth rings. With *carbon 14 (radiocarbon) dating* it is possible to make rough calculations of the time that has elapsed since the death of a living organism. Every living organism absorbs this radioactive carbon isotope contained in the atmosphere. When death occurs, this absorption ceases and the carbon 14 gradually vanishes. By chemical analysis of the carbon 14 retained in bones or charcoal, it is possible to date the time of death. With this method it is possible to assign dates as far back as 40.000 years or so. *Thermoluminescence,* last of all, is a method for dating fired clay, based on the changing distribution of electrons in a crystal, over time.

Prehistoric tool

The Pataud Shelter

Two Identity Cards

Neanderthal Man		**Cro-Magnon Man**
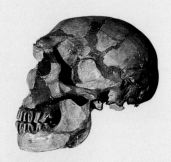		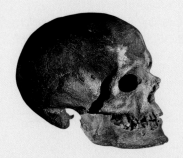
50.000 years ago	**Date of birth**	Approx. 30.000 years ago
European (data patchy)	**Lineage**	Worldwide (51,5 billion individuals in all, 6,5 billion currently living)
Hunter, gatherer	**Profession**	Hunter, fisherman, gatherer
La Ferrassie rock shelter (near Le Bugue) and other shelters	**Address**	Cro-Magnon rock shelter (Vézère valley) and other shelters
1,6 metres	**Height**	1,6 to 1,8 metres
Receding forehead Prominent brow-ridges Jaw pronounced No chin	**Distinguishing features**	Flat, receding forehead Jaw slight Pointed chin
Coarse	**Appearance**	Groomed
Cumbersome	**Gait**	Nimble
Average, practical (**Homo sapiens**)	**Intelligence**	Advanced (**Homo sapiens sapiens**)
Mousterian	**Culture**	Aurignacian, then Gravetian and Solutrean, lastly Magdalenian
Game, plants	**Diet**	Game (reindeer), fish, plants
Leather and fur?	**Clothing**	Refined: anoraks, trousers and moccasins made of stitched hide
None	**Ornaments, bone jewellery**	Wide range of stone knick-knacks
None	**Artistic activity**	Graphic arts, music
Not known, but buries dead	**Religion(s)**	Buries dead, decorates sanctuary caves
Flint sliver (scrapers, awls) and biface	**Stone tools**	Flint blades (blades, burins, scrapers, perforators)
None	**Bone tools - reindeer horn weapons**	Spears, harpoons, spear throwers, pierced sticks

B. and G. D.

traces, discovered at La Micoque site near Les Eyzies, provide evidence of settlements here some 350.000 years ago. From this point on, time is no longer reckoned in millions of years – not an easy scale to grasp – but in thousands of springs. Although in prehistory dates are of necessity imprecise, 100.000 to 200.000 years separate us from the appearance of Neanderthal man, also known as Mousterian man, a *Homo sapiens*, he was already something of a "scholar", even if his receding chin and low forehead gave him a slightly rough-and-ready facial aspect. In the prehistoric tradition, blatant injustice had labelled him a loutish brute, best avoided. A more humane type of justice would have Neanderthal man reclaim his dignity of an already well evolved man. His wide, elongated skull protected a brain equal in size to modern man's. He still fashioned biface flint slivers, but he also made scrapers, and tools with sharpened tips. He collected fossils and minerals for their appearance, buried his dead with much complex ceremony, which still eludes us. The sites of La Ferrassie and Régourdou contain evidence of all this in the form of human remains, pits and mounds, slabs of stone, and low dry-stone walling.The last Neanderthal men had the first *Homo sapiens sapiens* as their contemporaries – these most clever and informed men whose presence is attested in the Middle East 100.000 years ago. Thousands of years of technological evolution, slow to start with, but lightning swift in this modern age, have not significantly changed the general aspect of these remote forefathers. Their energy, their inventiveness and their manual dexterity turned them into a predominant group.

It was 35.000 years ago that *Homo sapiens sapiens* set up home in the Vézère valley, more specifically in the Cro-Magnon rock shelter. Fossil human remains were unearthed here, in the heart of Les Eyzies, in 1868, and the place has lent its name to this human type. Cro-Magnon man is frequently tall, with a

Prehistoric Nutrition

Whereas the first men and women fed themselves primarily with plants, the amount of meat in the human diet continued to increase as progress was made in the use of tools, attaining its highest percentage during the Upper Paleolithic with the civilization of great reindeer hunters. The image of the carnivorous caveman, forever in search of the animals which would have been his only food resource in a hostile, subzero environment, is a cliché which must be abandoned. It would mean too easily forgetting that these men belonged to the large family of *Homo sapiens sapiens* as we do, and that yesterday, as today, could not make do with a diet based exclusively on meat. In fact, although the amount of vegetation dropped by 20% during the coldest periods of the last glacier age, plants represented on average half the daily food intake of our ancestors. Work was divided up: hunting and fishing were reserved for the men while the women devoted themselves to gathering. Young roots, shoots, berries, nuts, and mushrooms along with meat and fish, provided a well-balanced diet. Would we have found a Cro-Magnon dish tasty, served without salt or spices? Different cooking methods allowed the plants to be easily chewed and assimilated while enhancing flavours and providing a variety of culinary pleasures. Our ancestors grilled, baked or steam-cooked and even boiled their food by dropping hot stones into cooking pots made of animal skins. But without a cookbook, the culinary arts of Prehistoric man, their particular way of combining foods and the correct proportioning of seasonings will forever remain a mystery.

high skull, straight forehead and well delineated chin. From now on, there is no difference between him and present-day man! The settlement of these human groups in the Perigord valleys, and the preservation of the fossilized remains of these people, have a miraculous quality to them. Henry Miller mentioned in his book *The Colossus of Maroussi* that he can find no good reason not to believe that if Cro-Magnon man settled in these parts, it was because he was extremely intelligent, and because he already had a highly developed sense of beauty. So was Cro-Magnon man attracted by the beauty of the setting or by the exceptionally favourable conditions for survival among these soaring cliffs, where frosts and thaws had taken turns to hew out canopies formed by mighty overhangs?

With a roof provided by nature, all he required was a small patch of more or less dry ground on which to lodge a few boughs against the rock face, and cover them with hides or furs. He elected to settle here in shelters at Pataud, La Madeleine, Cap-Blanc and Laugerie-Haute. To this day, all these sites have preserved the traces of Cro-Magnon man's everyday life: a refined and carefully fashioned range of tools – blades, pointed burins, scrapers, flint awls and perforators, spear and harpoon points and heads, and most noteworthy of all, those ingenious spear throwers capable of greatly increasing the power needed to hurl a spear or a javelin. Down the ages, the climate changed a great deal. Cro-Magnon man lived through the Würm glaciation, with its harsh winters marked by a Scandinavian-type climate. Tundra alternated with taiga over the years, in the coldest periods. Then, in the periods when the earth warmed again, moss and lichen, willow and dwarf birch gave way to pine– and birch-woods. The main animal resource was the reindeer, but there were plenty of other creatures too: mammoths, woolly rhinoceroses, horses, bison, aurochs, ibex, brown bears,

The Cap-Blanc Shelter: bison

A spear thrower's force

During the entire Paleolithic period, tools continued to evolve from the original carved stones of *Homo habilis*, in order to better respond to the various needs of human activity. Adapting to game and different hunting techniques, weapons became increasingly specialized, reaching an unprecedented diversity and efficiency with *Homo sapiens sapiens* during the Upper Paleolithic period. The range of materials used to make the weapons grew larger; in addition to the traditional flint, reindeer antler and bone were shaped and fitted together to create formidable assagai. Both the shape and amount of flint heads increased, showing great progress in increasingly efficient handle-fitting methods. But it is especially through the invention of new throwing techniques that *Homo sapiens sapiens'* ability reached its highest point.

Hunter using a spear thrower, Prehisto-Parc in Tursac

He invented the bow, quite a formidable weapon. But because he carved it out of wood, a perishable material, there are no examples dating earlier than the end of the Paleolithic period. Made out of reindeer antler, a more durable material, the spear thrower also provided an increase in throwing power. Still in use in Australia, its technique is well-known. It ressembles a stick with a hook against which is pressed the heel of the weapon, the assagai. To use it, the hunter draws his arm back and then propels the weapon forward. Kept in hand, the spearthrower works by a clever system of levers that improve the assagai's speed and precision. It is an efficient weapon, but it can also be considered an aesthetic object, for the Magdalenian man, both artist and engineer, enhanced its appearance by covering it with delicate carvings of animal silhouettes.

Spear thrower called Fawn with Birds, carved from a reindeer antler

Perigord Prehistory: An Outline

Time (B.C.)	Period	Culture	Human type	Human fossils	Site (* visible stratigraphy)	Activity (start of)	Tool range (start of)	Decorated shelters	Decorated caves
0	Iron Bronze					Sedentary settlement Dolmens Agriculture Livestock-farming	Metal tools	None in Perigord	
5.000	NEO-LI-THIC						Ceramics Polished stone tools		
	MESO-LI-THIC			Rochereil			Microliths		Teyjat Saint-Cirq Rouffignac Les Combarelles Font-de-Gaume Bara-Bahau Villars Lascaux
10.000		MAGDALENIAN		Chancelade La Madeleine	Reverdit* — Les Marseilles* (Laugerie-Basse) — La Madeleine — Chancelade			Cap-Blanc Reverdit	
15.000	UPPER PALAEOLITHIC	SOLUTREAN	HOMO SAPIENS SAPIENS / CRO-MAGNON MAN		Movius — Laugerie-Haute*			Fourneau du Diable Movius	La Grèze
20.000				Pataud		Sewing / Fishing		Pataud	
25.000		GRAVETTIAN		Cro-Magnon	Pataud* — La Gravette		Tools made of bone or reindeer horn, and bladed flint tools	Le Poisson Laussel	Pair-non-Pair (33)
30.000		AURIGNACIAN		Combe-Capelle	La Ferrassie* — Cro-Magnon	Art Jewellery		La Ferrassie Blanchard	Chauvet (07)
40.000				La Ferrassie Le Moustier	Le Moustier*				
	MIDDLE PALAEOLITHIC	MOUSTERIAN CULTURES	HOMO SAPIENS / NEANDERTHAL MAN	Roc Marsal		Burials			
				Le Régourdou					
100.000					La Micoque*		Tools made of flint slivers		
500.000	LOWER PALAEOLITHIC	ACHEULIAN	HOMO ERECTUS	Tautavel (66)		Fire (controlled)	Biface tools		
1 m. yrs									
1,5 m. yrs			HOMO HABILIS	Olduvaï (Afrique)		Hunting Gathering	Worked pebbles		
2 m. yrs			AUSTRA-LOPI-THECUS						
3 m. yrs				Lucy (Africa)			No tools		B. and G. D.

various members of the cat family, foxes and ptarmigans. Last but not least, Cro-Magnon man was the undisputed artist of the Paleolithic era, the prime mover of a cultural revolution. It was he who invented drawing, achieving a spectacular intellectual advance. By now, he was capable of creating two-dimensional reproductions of three-dimensional figures observed in the wild, and transferring them on to the walls of shelters and deep caves. This cave art, be it drawing, painting, carving or sculpture, together with the known range of smaller art objects, offers ample evidence of his mastery of line and colour. Lascaux is superb, but it is certainly not in a class of its own. Not unlike an art gallery, the Dordogne, Beune and Vézère valleys display a dazzling array of works. Suffice it to mention the decorated sanctuary caves of Font-de-Gaume, Les Combarelles, Rouffignac, Bara-Bahau, Saint-Cirq, Cap-Blanc, Bernifal and Villars – an impressive list indeed, but by no means exhaustive.

Eponymous Sites

Land of man's beginnings, Perigord was also a land of prehistoric science. What could be better proof than the names of several Paleolithic cultures which have retained the name of their Perigourdian origin? They are eponymous sites (from the Greek word *epônumos*, that which names) and the tools unearthed there helped identify, define and classify prehistoric cultures: the Mousterian (from Le Moustier), the Perigourdian, the Gravetian (La Gravette in Bayac) and the Magdalenian (La Madeleine in Tursac) as well as more specific types such as the Tayacian and the Micoquian (La Micoque in Eyzies-de-Tayac) or the subclassification of the Ferrassie type of Mousterian. Finally, it is difficult to forget that the most famous *Homo sapiens sapiens*, Cro-Magnon, owes his name to a rock shelter in the village of Eyzies.

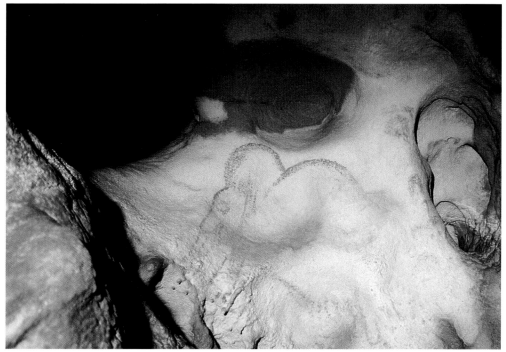

Bernifal Cave: a mammouth drawn in clay

The Art of the Great Hunters

Neolithic cave painting was born some 35.000 years ago, on the banks of the Vézère and Ardèche Rivers. In a land of limestone, riddled with caves and rock shelters, Cro-Magnon man developed his stylized depictions of animals interspersed with other marks and geometric signs which are still poorly explained. These drawings, be they realistic or symbolic, invariably occur on easily accessible rock walls, illuminated by natural daylight. In Perigord this was the apprenticeship period, associated with the oldest strata of the Aurignacien, Gravetian and Solutrean cultures. It was not until the "Lascaux period", 17.000 years ago, that men decided to venture into the dark and dreaded depths of large caves. They drew on walls never touched by natural light. We must go with the evidence: those people invented their own lighting – rudimentary but efficient lamps

fuelled with fat or tallow. The best known such lamp is a magnificent pink sandstone specimen found near the Well Gallery at Lascaux. It consists of a small round 'bowl' and a handle carved with oblique and parallel signs, a Lascaux hallmark. The bold-stroked animal figures – horses, aurochs and bison – are always accompanied by enigmatic geometric signs – circles, ovals, rectangles, and rows of lines, dots and dashes. The animals, which appear to be suspended on the walls, are not depicted amidst any scenery which might suggest the nature of the ground or the topography of the countryside. There is no sun or moon, no clouds, no plantlife, no depiction of familiar objects. This outstanding mastery of form and graphic expression blossomed further with the Magdalenian culture. And it also vanished with it, some 10.000 years ago, when the last Ice Age drew to an end. Of the various forms of artistic expression developed by man in the Upper Paleolithic, we only have evidence of the three techniques requiring

Reindeer, carved on a bone blade, Magdalenian Period, from the Morin Shelter

Red and black cow and small horses, Lascaux Cave

schist palettes, grinders, pestles, and bowls. The Magdalenian people were fond of decorating walls deep inside their caves, but they also wore ornaments made with seashells, bone and animal teeth. The discovery at Lascaux of fifteen pieces of unmistakable jewellery – seashells pierced with tiny apertures so that they could be suspended – was of paramount importance, because it confirms the level of evolution of these groups of men and women, already inclined to take an interest in their appearance by showing a coquettish soft spot for finery, unless these objects served as amulets.

a more or less permanent rock or bone surface: painting, carving and sculpture. Sculpture is the rarest, and engraving the simplest, calling for no more than a sharp-pointed tool to chisel the rock. Sometimes these people used just their fingers, if the surface was particularly soft. Painting required a much more elaborate technique. A suitable ground had to be chosen, and a palette of, if possible, indelible dyes prepared. Once worked and mixed, these mineral dyes could be broken down to produce twenty or so different hues, ranging from pale yellow to reddish-brown to the darkest black. Yellow ochre was the most widespread, being used in the natural state or else oxidized into a very bright red by roasting. The orange-red colour was obtained from haematite, a natural ferrous oxide. White was made from a base of calcite or kaolin. The manganese dioxide that decomposes in caves produced dark hues in the black range. The palette had neither greens nor blues! All these colours were stabilized by a bonding agent, the limestone-rich water peculiar to the caves and caverns in these parts. There is something more stirring still about the objects, unearthed at Lascaux, used to prepare the actual paints: limestone or

Venus with a Horn, from the prehistoric deposit of Laussel, Gravetian Period

29

3

FROM VESONA TO THE DORDOGNE

The Neolithic period, dating back to around 7.000 B.C. (also known as the age of polished stone) was the time of agriculture, animal breeding and human settlement. People tilled the land, harvested and conserved the fruits of their labour. They gathered in villages where they made tools of ceramics, bronze, iron as well as weaving on looms. Dolmens, such as Blanc near Beaumont, Brantôme or Paussac, remind us that Neolithic people buried their dead under huge *tumuli* of stone and earth. The use of copper and more complex alloys like bronze to make tools and jewellery is attested in Perigord in the third millennium B.C.

Man then entered the modern historical period. Metalworking and ceramics were improved and refined. Perigord was the territory of the Gallic tribes called Petrocorii, meaning four tribes or four armies. With the Roman conquest, Perigord entered the Gallo-Roman period. The Petrocorii acquired a handsome capital, *Vesona*, now Périgueux. Vast estates, opulent *villæ*, enhanced the countryside. This period of prosperity and peace, the *Pax Romana*, bequeathed many a place-name ending in -ac, -at, -as, and -an, the monuments of Vesona and the mosaics in the Gallo-Roman villa of Montcaret.

But the Roman empire started to buckle under the Barbarian invasions. The inhabitants took refuge behind the walls of Vesona, hastily erected with the stones of dismantled Roman buildings, and the land fell into the hands of the Visigoths, whose capital was Toulouse.

In 507, at Vouillé, Clovis clinched his victory over Gaul and Perigord came under the sway of the Franks. Since Clovis's conversion to Christianity in 496, this religion had developed rapidly in Perigord. Monasticism was active and, in the 7th century, abbeys like Brantôme and Le Puy-Saint Front were built. But subsequent Barbarian invasions lay in store for Perig-

Stone Table

According to the definition provided by Dr. Jean Arnal: "The dolmen is an open tomb-like chamber, generally megalithic, covered over by a burial mound, or tumulus, and intended to receive several burials." The word commonly used to designate this monument is composed of two Breton words: *dol* and *men,* which mean table and stone, respectively. Certainly, this metaphor illustrates what remains of the dolmen when freed of the covering of earth and stones which make up the burial mound. There are three types of dolmens: the passage dolmen, where the funerary chamber opens to the outside by way of a corridor; the gallery dolmen, where the corridor and the chamber are barely differentiated; and the plain dolmen, which opens directly to the outside. Ceremonies were also held around the dolmen to celebrate the cult of the dead and the Neolithic communities' bond with their land.

The Blanc Gallery near Beaumont

ord. During the 9th century, the Norsemen made their way up the Dordogne and Vézère rivers with their shallow-draught vessels. They burnt churches and monasteries, and looted towns. Périgueux was not spared. Strongholds were built to combat them, perched on high ground or built in cliff-faces, as at La Roque-Saint-Christophe. In due course people organized themselves, no longer expecting aid from a distant royal power. They put up local defences, founded on loyal obedience to those who could offer protection – the noble families. The 10th century saw the creation of the four Perigord baronies – Mareuil, Bourdeilles, Beynac and Biron – which have bequeathed us castles where, in the 12th and 13th centuries, troubadours like Bertran de Born or Arnaud de Mareuil sang of *fine amour*. Churches like those at Saint-Amand-de-Coly, Tayac and Trémolat were fortified and the abbeys of Cadouin, Sarlat, Boschaud and Chancelade all played an active part in developing the region's agricultural base.

As a borderland between the French Capetians and the English Plantagenets, Perigord switched from one jurisdiction to the other. The 13th century was a period of prosperity and expansion, marked by the erection of striking churches, the development of towns such as Sarlat, Périgueux and Bergerac, and the construction of some twenty fortified bastides, French-style as at Domme, Villefranche-du-Perigord and Eymet, or English, as at Monpazier, Beaumont and Lalinde. But the Hundred Years' War smouldered in the problems of succession of King Philip IV the Fair. His legitimate grandson, Edward III of England, claimed his due. By his mother Isabella, daughter of Philip IV, he laid claim to the vacant French throne. Needless to add, another Philip, a mere nephew, was summoned to take power under the name of Philip VI (the first Valois king). But the English pretender denied him the right to reign over the French regions. Thus started the fearful trials of war, aggravated by those other two scourges of God,

Bertran de Born

Lord and troubadour, Bertran de Born (1140-1205) put as much talent into singing about love as fighting in battle. Capable of profundity in his religious and political thoughts and refinement in his evocations of love, Bertran, as the perfect knight, also loved weapons and bravery. Didn't he say, "I feel joy when I see the horses and armed riders line up on the field"? When Richard the Lionheart deprived him of his family castle in Hautefort, bestowing it instead upon his brother Constantin, he took part in the infighting between the Plantagenets. Although he sided with Prince Henry against Henry II and Richard the Lionheart, he ended up rallying to the latter's cause. He was at Richard's side when the chateau of Chalus in Limousin was beseiged in 1199 and the English sovereign was killed by the bolt of a crossbow. Dante wrote of him in his *Inferno*, aimlessly wandering, his head held out in his hands like a lantern for having turned the Plantegenet father and son into enemies. And yet, this warrior-poet retired to the Cistercian abbey in Dalon, leaving behind forty or so plays written in the Occitan language, along with love songs and *sirventes*, in which the full force of his satirical verve is pure pleasure to the reader.

Hautefort Castle

Perigord Personalities – some native, some adopted

Le Moustier or Mousterian Man (also called Neanderthal Man), around 50.000 years ago

Cro-Magnon Man, 30.000 years ago, Les Eyzies

Jérôme de Périgueux (d. 1120), bishop, companion of El Cid

Bertran de Born (1140-1215), troubadour and soldier, Hautefort

Charles de Biron (1562-1602), companion to Henri IV, Marshal of France, beheaded for treason

Etienne de La Boétie (1530-1563), writer, friend of Montaigne, Sarlat

Montaigne (1533-1592), writer and thinker (*Essays*)

Brantôme (Pierre de Bourdeille, Abbot of) (1540-1614), chronicler (*The Gallant Ladies*) and soldier

Marie d'Hautefort (1616-1691), (platonic) beloved of Louis XIII

Fénelon (1651-1715), prelate, tutor to the Duke of Burgundy and author of *Telemachus*, Salignac

Monseigneur Christophe de Beaumont (1703-1781), Archbishop of Paris, Meyrals

Henri Bertin (1719-1792), Comptroller General of Finance and minister of Louis XV, Bourdeilles

Talleyrand (Charles Maurice de Talleyrand-Perigord) (1754-1838), bishop, then minister and diplomat

Joseph Joubert (1754-1824), moralist (*Reflections*), friend of Chateaubriand, Montignac

Maine de Biran (1766-1824), philosopher, Bergerac

Pierre Daumesnil (1777-1832), one-legged general and Vincennes defender in1814 and in1830

Bugeaud (1784-1849), Marshal of France, Governor-General of Algeria and farmer, Lanouaille

Pierre Magne (1806-1879), minister of Napoléon III, Trélissac

Orélie Antoine de Tounens (1825-1878), lawyer in Périgueux, then king elect of Araucania and Patagonia, Tourtoirac and Chourgnac-d'Ans

Eugène Le Roy (1836-1907), regionalist novelist (*Jacquou le Croquant*), Montignac and Hautefort

Rachilde (1860-1953), novelist, co-founder of *Mercure de France*, Château-l'Évêque

Charles de Foucauld (1858-1916), officer, explorer and then hermit, Bergerac

Sem (Georges Goursat) (1863-1934), cartoonist and caricaturist, Périgueux

Denis Peyrony (1869-1954), prehistorian, Les Eyzies

André Maurois (1885-1967), novelist and biographer, Excideuil

Louis Delluc (1890-1924), man of letters, critic and film-maker, Cadouin

Gaston Ouvrard (1890-1981), comic singer, Cadouin and Couze

Josephine Baker (1906-1975), variety artist, Les Milandes

B. and G. D.

famine and plague! Perigord and the kingdom of France suffered similar agonies.

The early 16th century ushered in a flourishing period, influenced by the Italian Renaissance in the civil, military, and ecclesiastical architecture of Perigord. But this was no more than a brief truce in the history of this province.

Perigord was split squarely into two enemy camps during the Wars of Religion, Périgueux being Catholic and Bergerac Calvinist. The tragic revolt of the *Croquants* took place in 1595. The region did not regain its stability until 1607, when it was linked once and for all to the kingdom of France. But it was only a relative stability, punctuated by outbursts of restlessness, turmoil and commotion, like the great conflagration across the land in 1637. The brutal application of a most ill-conceived royal order, decreeing an extraordinary levying of corn to feed the troops, triggered an uprising among the peasantry, already being squeezed by dues, taxes, rates and other du-

ties. Led by a gentleman named La Mothe-La Forêt, a veritable army of peasants, several thousand strong, marched on Périgueux, and even managed to force their way into Bergerac on May 11, 1637. Had Sainte-Foy-la-Grande not put up firm resistance and stopped the army's onward rush in its stride, it would have attempted to occupy Bordeaux. The peasants were forced to disperse, but anger still ran high, and guerilla tactics instilled a climate of rumbling bitterness and latent violence across the Perigord countryside until 1642, when the monarchy finally managed to restore order. The 18th century was one hallmarked by social and sometimes economic tension, which endured right up until the Revolution. Perigord then became the *département* of the Dordogne. It is not a large region, it attracts few headlines, and is not easy to pinpoint on the map. But visitors with an interest in history and prehistory are helping to bring a certain vitality back to the area, which proudly boasts the title of "Land of Man's Beginnings".

Bergerac: houses in the Rue des Rois

Bastides, medieval "new towns"

During the 12th century, the Church created *sauvetés*, or sanctuary lands, in order to promote God's peace. A *sauveté* could become a *villeneuve*, a new town, and benefit from tax exemption or tax relief which allowed a deserted or unsafe region to be occupied and an economic centre to be set up and put into operation. In the 13th and 14th centuries, in Aquitaine and Languedoc, more and more bastides developed as of 1222, the year one was founded in Cordes, near Albi, by Raymond VII of Toulouse. For their founders, bastides were a means to derive rights and revenue but they also provided better control by regrouping population. Situating the new towns on the border of their lands provided defense as well. A writ or deed of partition and a

Eymet: Place des Arcades

Molières: the church

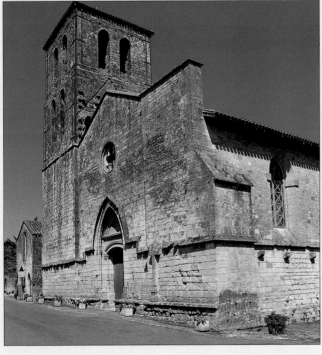

Customary charter always preceded the foundation of a bastide. By the former, a civil or ecclesiastical landowner gave up his land to royal or noble agents, who then took charge of populating the bastide. The charter promised security and the possibility of success to new arrivals, sometimes specifying the dimensions of land plots and the organization of public highways, cart roads or crossways and alleys. After Raymond VII's death, the new count of Toulouse, Alphonse de Poitiers, founded no less than thirty-six bastides, such as Eymet in Perigord, where the Plantagenets created those of Beaumont, Monpazier and Molières. Generally, a bastide was built on an orthogonal layout around a square bordered with walkways, often with a covered market. Its streets were laid out like a checkerboard. The four consuls, elected each year to govern the bastide, sat at the commonhouse found on the square or sometimes under the covered market. A church, built in the Gothic style and partly financed by donations from its inhabitants, was a symbol of their town's prosperity.

Domme: Del Bos fortified gate

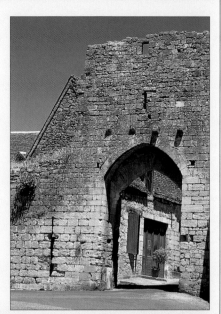

Monpazier: market hall

2

ITINERARIES

1

AROUND MONPAZIER

Besse

Located about ten kilometres north of the bastide of Villefranche-du-Perigord, founded by Alphonse of Poitiers, Besse has retained its 11th-12th century Romanesque church, whose chevet and transept were built in the 15th century. With its high square, squat nave, its thick blind walls, and its *lauze*-covered roof, the church is visibly fortified. Like in many churches in Perigord, access to the inside of Besse church is through an imposing porch-belltower which overlooks the 11th century portal. Three semi-circular, sculpted voussoirs are set above the door. The sculptures on the central voussoir are particularly remarkable: they show Isaiah holding a book, and Adam and Eve trying to hide their nudity, around the tree of life. Then the same clothed figures are shown while the serpent winds around the tree. On the right, the legend of Saint Eustache is presented. A hunter on horseback shoots an arrow at a stag, between whose antlers a tiny figure is none other than Jesus Christ. Another image shows the Virgin and Child, while yet another, Saint Michael. The voussoir of the intrados is carved with palms framing the Easter Lamb at the top. These two voussoirs drop down onto carved capitals, including one with figures of men, monsters and demons. A cornice tops the portal, resting on six sculpted modillions representing, among others, a monster, an animal tamer and contortionists.

Besse: the church chevet

Biron

As early as the 11th century, a fortified castle was built on top of the verdant knoll called Biron, which was the seat of one of the four baronies of Perigord along with Bourdeilles, Mareuil and Beynac. In 1212, the medieval fortress was severely damaged by the violent onslaughts of Simon de Montfort's crusaders. The commander of the Albigensian crusade against the Cathars had just captured Penne d'Agenais, held by Hugues d'Alfaro, son-in-law of Raymond VI, after eight weeks of siege. The defender Martin Algaï, himself a devout Cathar, shut himself away in the beseiged stronghold. Then he surrendered to his executioners to save his own people before suffering a dramatic death – he was dragged along behind a horse before being hanged.

At the end of 15th and the beginning of the 16th century, under the energetic auspices of its lord Pons de Gontaut-Biron and his descendants the castle developed into a monumental complex. The chapel dates from this time. Construction was interrupted at the beginning of the 17th century after Charles de Gontaut-Biron's execution and taken up again from 1715 to 1730.

To access the lower courtyard one must first pass the inspection of a guard-tower, with a Renaissance doorway with ogee sculpting. Close by, the walls of the 16th century chapel are reinforced by buttresses. Along the top runs a pierced balustrade hugging every contour of the structure. An onion-shaped bell-tower astride the steeply pitched roof rounds off the building. The nave has two stories, and the upper floor, level with the courtyard, houses the castle chapel by cunning use of the different levels of the terrain. The lower floor, accessible from the village, was the parish church. Two fine, if somewhat mutilated, sculpted recumbent tomb figures guard the remains of two of the most famous lords of Biron, Pons and Armand de Gontaut-Biron. In the north-

The "Gontaut-Biron"

For eight centuries, Biron castle has belonged to one family: the Gontaut. From the 12th to the 20th century, fourteen generations have followed one another, contributing to their house's renown through deeds or misdeeds their house's renown. During the Hundred Years War, the Gontaut sided either with the king of England or the French crown, depending on the circumstances. However, beginning in the 15th century, the first barons of Perigord became the faithful servants of the French monarchy and proved their valiance in the royal armies. Former chamberlain of Henri III, Pons followed the king on his campaigns in Italy while his brother, Armand, was bishop of Sarlat from 1492 to 1519. Another Armand was ambassador to Piedmont, then Commanding Officer of the Bastille and Grand Master of Artillery. He married his daughters to Protestant lords, without for all that betraying Henri III, nor his successor Henri IV. In 1592, he died in the battle of Epernay; his son, Charles, displaying his thirty-two wounds like trophies, entered into Henri IV's confidence. The king decided to reward the one who had served him with such courage. His barony was promoted to the rank of peerage-duchy, and Charles was made an admiral, Marshal of France, lieutenant general of the Armies and Governor of Burgandy. So many honours! Too many honours? Charles was insatiable. His lightning rise in stature went to his head and he plotted against the one man to whom he owed all. The first plot was pardoned by the good king; a second plot, the king was prepared to pardon but Biron had to confess. Too sure of himself, too proud, he refused. Henri IV could not yield. For the crime of high treason, the executioner's axe flashed on the July 31, 1602, within the walls of the Bastille.

ernmost part, the outer courtyard is delimited by the slightly severe building housing the "Collector's Office", the *Recette*. Peasants would line up here to pay heavy dues, be it with money or in kind, true symbols of the way these lords held sway over their lands. Access to the court of honour is through a stairway followed by a vaulted passage. To the north, the 16th century lord's residence is next to the long 12th century keep; to the south, another main building, built in several stages from the 16th to the 18th centuries, houses, on the first floor, the timbered Great Hall of the States General. Henri IV's tower stands on its western corner. The yard opens out through a depressed arch on a magnificent columned portico reached via a flight of steps that sweep up the principal stairway. Beyond lie the lawned slopes of the gardens and park. The tiny village that encircles the castle has several fine Renaissance residences, the most famous of which is called the Bernard Palissy House, where the brilliant ceramist is said to have lived.

Biron Castle: the guard-tower's Renaissance door

Biron Castle: timber-work in the Great Hall of the States General

Monpazier

Monpazier is an archetypal medieval *bastide*, re-taining nearly intact all the distinctive features. It was founded on January 7, 1284 by Edward I of England, on this occasion in association with Pierre Gontaut, lord of the neighbouring castle of Biron, to guard the great thorough-fare linking the Agen region and Perigord. The carefully conceived layout, die-straight, forms an oblong 400 metres long by 220 metres wide. The main streets, running perpendicular, divide up the town like a chequer-board. By decree, every inhabitant was given a strictly calculated parcel. Houses had to be built within a maximum length of 20 metres with a 8 metre wide façade giving on to the street. A space called an *androne* ran between each par-cel, acting as a fire-break in an age when fires were a scourge not easy to combat. The *an-drone* was also used as a garbage dump, be-cause, in those days, public health and hygiene were not yet an overriding concern of the citi-zenry. The open arcades below the houses, *cornières*, surrounding the main square offer a cool refuge. These "covered walks" contrast sharply with the broad, open quality of the square, throbbing with heat, where scarlet, vel-vety roses complement the pale hues of the buildings.
The market, with superb beams and rafters, supported by small stonework pillars, con-tains ancient measures for weighing walnuts and chestnuts, attesting to the time-honoured wealth that Perigord managed to derive from its splendid forests.
Work on the church of Saint Dominic started in the 13th century. It has since been soundly altered, with each period and century adding its particular style. Its bell-tower is aligned with the extension of the façade. The church was built away from the square, as was cus-tomary in bastides. A beautiful rose window crowns the main door, in turn surrounded by semi-circular voussoirs. The small town,

well-protected behind its walls, punctuated by six fortified gateways of which three remain, offered too many strategic advantages to be overlooked by the bloody Hundred Years War. First English, then French, then English again, it underwent a whirl of sieges and plun-der and violence, accompanied of course, by a procession of disastrous epidemics, typhoid fever or plague. Betrayed during the Wars of Religion, in 1574 Monpazier fell into the hands of the Huguenot captain Geoffroy de Vivans. Twenty years later, it survived the first uprising of the *Croquants*, peasant revo-lutionaries of Perigord exasperated by the ever more onerous burden of taxes and the ar-rogance of the nobility. In the thick of the 17th century, the peasant revolt led by Buf-farot, a weaver from the nearby town of Cap-drot, culminated in dreadful repression. The ringleader was arrested and sentenced to the vilest of deaths: he was drawn and quartered in the main square of Monpazier on August 16, 1637.

Monpazier: the church of Saint Dominic

Saint-Avit-Sénieur and Beaumont

Situated on the edge of Bessède forest, Saint-Avit-Sénieur is a tiny village dominated by the huge bulk of its fortified church, the former abbey church of an Augustinian foundation that, in 1097, depended on Saint-Sernin of Toulouse. Geraud of Sales was a canon here before becoming a wandering hermit whose disciples founded the Abbey of Cadouin in 1115. In 1118, the mortal remains of Saint Avit were placed in the church. Fortified in the 14th century, it was intended to serve as a refuge for people from towns unable to find a proper stronghold. The parapet walk, crenellations, the windowless 'blind' walls and stout towers flanking the façade, all contribute to the multi-purpose nature of the building. Part fortress, part place of worship, its architecture wavers between these two styles. The result is a most original edifice. The scant remains of the cloister and abbey buildings – the monks' dormitory and a chapter-house – adjoining the church have been invaded by grass, but they still evoke powerful memories. The splendour of past centuries is summed up in these beautiful stones.

Saint-Avit-Sénieur lies halfway between two English bastides, Molières to the north, and Beaumont to the west. Founded in 1272 by a Seneschal of Guyenne, Beaumont today contains just a few houses with arcaded galleries, traces of its old town walls with the Luzier gate and, its huge Saint-Front fortified church. Four corner towers with bare, windowless walls reinforce the buttressed building, and a parapet walk runs round the whole edifice. Even the solid transept resembles an additional fortification. The only graceful feature permitted this religious fortress is an elegant façade, embellished by a Gothic doorway above which runs a gallery with a finely carved balustrade.

Beaumont: Luzier Door

Geraud of Sales

At the end of the 11th century, in the continuation of the Gregorian reform, the world of monasticism found renewed interest in the eremitic life. Geraud of Sales, who had been a canon at Saint-Avit-Senieur in his youth, became a wandering hermit in Perigord. From 1113 to 1114, he travelled to every corner of Aquitaine and rallied many disciples to his cause, some of whom would found the Abbey of Cadouin in 1115. For women, he recommended the frontevraud model; for men, he created hermitages which he often visited. Before his death in 1120, ever faithful to his eremitic vocation but conscious of the practical difficulties it entailed and the spread of coenobitism, he advised his disciples to adopt Saint Benedict's rule "in the spirit of the Cistercians".

2

HEADING UP THE DORDOGNE VALLEY

Montcaret

In the small valley where Montcaret lies sheltered between the hills of Montravel and Le Platan, overlooking the Dordogne valley, human settlements are attested in prehistoric times. Its 11th century Romanesque church was built by Benedictine monks. In the semi-dome apse, the arcatures rest on five columns some of whose capitals are Romanesque and pre-Romanesque. Archeological excavations undertaken around the church have unearthed an impressive Gallo-Roman vestiges of *villa*. A handsome courtyard complete with peristyle has been cleared, as well as a whole series of rooms clearly designed for bathing. Hypocausts, underground heating systems in which hot air circulated, are clearly visible with their small supporting brick pillars. Hot rooms (*caldarium*), warm rooms (*tepidarium*) and cold rooms (*frigidarium*) are decorated with beautiful 4th century Pyrenean marble and superb mosaics, discovered in 1884. The tesserae – tiny cubes cut from different coloured rocks – form an infinite series of geometric and stylized patterns: crosses, coils, wreaths, stripes and rosettes decorate a pool with aquatic designs of fish, shells and octopus. A later mosaic, possibly Merovingian, has been unearthed to the north of the church. An on-site museum protects certain mosaics and displays finds such as Roman capitals and funerary furnishings – a reminder that, from the 5th to the 12th centuries, this was a burial ground.

Montcaret: Gallo-Roman mosaics from the 4th century

Saint-Michel-de-Montaigne

Of the medieval residence acquired by the Eyquem de Montaigne family in 1477, virtually nothing now remains in the wake of a tragic fire that destroyed the main structure in 1884. But the fire did spare what, in the eyes of Michel de Montaigne, was the most celebrated part of his castle – the famous "library tower" where he wrote his *Essays*. The manor was a hybrid between a fortress and a fortified farm. The long buildings – still standing – which form a four-sided yard attest to this. A massive tower with narrow windows stood at each corner.To avoid the bustle and worry of family life, Michel de Montaigne elected to turn one of these towers, part mill and part dovecote, into a haven of peace where he could think, muse, and write. The first room you enter in the tower is a chapel that has certainly been touched up, apart from a fresco painted in the recess formed by the choir and which Montaigne himself mentions. The master's bedchamber is just above. An aperture in the wall enabled Montaigne to follow mass without having to descend a spiral staircase, awkward for an elderly man, not in the best of health. The uppermost floor, lastly, houses Montaigne's famous "library". In his *Essays*, he describes in great detail the room where he felt most at home. It is round, well-lit, and was originally lined with books arrayed on shelves. On the beams holding up the ceiling Montaigne had inscribed, in handsome block lettering, maxims and axioms chosen from the ancient writings of Greek and Latin authors. Every so often he would erase them and have new dicta inscribed. As a place of contemplation, work and prayer, the tower is still imbued with the presence of the philosopher, even if much of the furniture belonging to him is no longer there. The house is surrounded by magnificent gardens, with lawns shaped like clover leaves – emblem of the Montaignes.

Montaigne

Michel Eyquem was born in 1533 in Montaigne Castle. He studied law as a student at the Guyenne school in Bordeaux. As a consultant at the Parliament of Bordeaux, he became friends with Étienne de La Boétie. In 1571, he published the works of La Boétie, who had died in 1563. Having withdrawn to his "library", he began writing his *Essays* which were first published in two volumes in Bordeaux in 1580.

That same year he made trips to Italy, Switzerland and Germany to take the thermal waters as a cure for the gravel that kept him in constant pain. But these trips also allowed him to distance himself from a France in the throes of the Wars of Religion. He was elected mayor of Bordeaux upon his return in 1581. During his term, he served as a mediator between the king of France and Henri de Navarre. After 1586, he began writing a new edition of the *Essays*. Here are a few excerpts:

On his upbringing:

"It was an inviolable rule that, in my company, himself [his father] and my mother, valets and chambermaids should speak only in those words of Latin that each had learnt to jabber with me"..."As for me, I was more than six years old before I understood as much French or Perigord dialect as Arabic.

"On his library:

"It is on the third floor of a tower. In it I spend most days of my life, and most hours of each day. The form is round, the only flat surface being that required for my table and chair. At one glance, I can survey all my books arranged at an angle of 5 degrees all around."

On his friendship with Etienne de la Boétie:

"If I am pressed to say why I loved him, I feel the only response can be thus: `Because he was he, and I was me."

Bergerac

The enchanting walled town of Bergerac lies in the middle of a small alluvial plain, where the Dordogne river meanders its gentle way westward. The town was first built on this site in the Middle Ages, at a time when villagers would gather their homes around a fortified castle, the better to protect them against danger. During the 12th century, the construction of a bridge spanning the Dordogne turned this sprawling village into an important commercial centre. In those days, the river and the bridge across it were the town's life-lines. The Dordogne is navigable from the edge of the Auvergne in seasons of spate. As the years passed, it played host to ever more heavily laden barges chugging their cargoes between the Massif Central and Bordeaux. As for the bridge, it was the only permanent and safe crossing over the temperamental Dordogne. Wealth brings with it culture, and Bergerac became an intellectual centre where burgeoning Calvinism would find particularly fertile ground. By the 16th century Bergerac was one of the capitals of Protestantism. But this beacon town also fell victim to the latent animosity developing between Catholics and Protestants, soon to turn into fierce hatred. After the Revocation of the Edict of Nantes in 1685, many Protestant townsfolk, disenchanted by the monarchy's less than amiable attitude, preferred to seek exile in the distant United Provinces of the Netherlands, and abandoned their handsome town. Even if Bergerac, not without a pang of jealousy, saw Périgueux hang onto its status of 'county town' when the *départements* were created in 1791, the town prospered during the 18th and 19th centuries. In this period, Bergerac was rated as one of France's major ports. The town's wealth was built on inland water transport, cooperage and tobacco. Then the advent of the railway, on the one hand, and the devastating phylloxera pest on the other combined to ruin the thriving economy of this entire region. Today, Bergerac

Wine, Cooperage and River Craft

As a centre of wine production and an important port on the Dordogne River, it was natural that Bergerac dedicate a museum to wine and river craft. Located in a fine half-timbered building dating from the 18th century, giving onto the Place de la Myrpe that once had a tavern for boatmen, the collections of the Museum of Wine and River Craft evoke the life of people from Bergerac and their town linked to these two economic activities. On the second floor, a complete picture of winemaking traditions is provided by old photographs, maps and old tools used by the wine producers and coopers of the Bergerac area. There were numerous *barricayres*, makers of the barrels used to transport wine, in Bergerac, which contained several dozen workshops just before the French Revolution. The museum pays tribute to them by presenting the various stages of their work. On the third floor, the essential element in the development of wine production – transportation by river and canal – is approached with, in particular, models of the boats traditionally used on the Dordogne, the flat-bottomed *gabares* and hulled *courreaux*, that used to carry wine from the Bergerac area to Bordeaux. The biggest of these vessels, 25 metres long, were able to transport up to 100 barrels. The ground floor of the museum, containing a temporary exhibition hall, contains a fine 18th century washing-tub.

A *gabare*

is a small busy town, and seat of the National Tobacco Institute, which makes it France's tobacco – or rather *tabak* – capital. And its fully revived vineyards now produce a sought-after AOC wine, boasting such famous labels as Bergerac, Montravel, Pécharmant, Rosette, Saussignac and Monbazillac.

The old town crowds around the cobbled embankment that runs gently down to the water's edge. Here, let your mind's eye imagine barges at moorings, plump barrels being rolled rowdily to and fro, bargees yelling, and all the hustle and bustle of a whole *quartier* now becalmed. The ancient streets nearby are lined with fine half-timbered houses, their cantilevered façades surveying splendid vaulted carriage gateways. Rue d'Albret, rue Saint-James, rue des Fontaines, all set in a maze of lanes where traces of bygone days abound. At the foot of the beautiful church of Saint James, a staging-post on the pilgrimage to Compostela, Pélissière Square, with its rows of steps, has a pretty, circular fountain. Myrpe

Bergerac: Peyrarède House

Bergerac: Myrpe Square

Square is lined with half-timbered houses and boasts a very stark statue of Cyrano de Bergerac. He was not native to these parts, but tradition and legend have doggedly joined forces to exalt this literary phenomenon as a scion of this place. Built between the 12th and 17th centuries, the old Récollets monastery houses the Interprofessional Wine Board of the Bergerac Region. In the 17th century, the Récollets wanted to restore to their proper faith the townspeople who were overly drawn by the lure of the reformed church. Dragonnades, or strongarm methods used against Protestants to make them recant their faith, and bookburning gained momentum at the time of the Revocation of the Edict of Nantes. By a nice historical irony, a Protestant church has been built right next door, on the site of the old Notre Dame Church. The monastery also houses an oenological laboratory, and is the annual venue for meetings of the Conference of Wine Consuls in the ancient cellars, where the monks once made and laid down their wines.

Bergerac: Récollets Cloister

The Wine Crop

No, this is not some wild fair overflowing with the generous nectar of the wines made in and around Bergerac! *Vinée* comes from an old Latin word, *vinita*. In the Middle Ages, the *vinée* described the rural vine-growing area directly controlled by the community of Bergerac. There is plenty of evidence of vine-growing in the Dordogne valley dating back to the 12th century. Bergerac's wine merchants, supported by their consuls, were early promoters of conspicuous protectionism for a product that brought them both wealth and renown. They drew up rules and regulations, as well as some of the most draconian inspection procedures devised anywhere for this crop. Everything was clearly codified, and governed by a handful of energetic traders and brokers, resolved, come what may, to protect their privileges: the quality of the vines, the date of the grape-harvest, the obligation – for Monbazillac growers, at least – to wait until "noble rot" (botrytis) had finally produced the most advanced stage of ripeness, right of entry to the town, reserved exclusively to "*vinée* members" for the sale and dispatch of the precious beverage, and so on. The Wine Board and the *Vinée* consulship still keep a watchful eye on this product, and even if the vocabulary has been changed by advertising campaigns and marketing techniques, their prime concern is to promote the wines of Bergerac. The vintage wines of Bergerac may not enjoy the renown of those illustrious neighbouring clarets, but they certainly merit their *Appellation d'Origine Contrôlée*. The Bergerac *appellation* covers not only the famous wines of Monbazillac, Montravel and Pécharmant, but is also granted to dozens of villages producing an elegant light red wine, with a subtle bouquet, and often best drunk young.

The Tobacco Museum

The Renaissance-style Peyrarède Mansion, built in 1604, and once a private residence, now houses the Tobacco Museum. It displays the amazing history of this plant hailing from the New World, and introduced to France by one Jean Nicot (whence nicotine!), French ambassador to Portugal, who purveyed a few pinches of powder to Catherine de' Medici to help relieve her migraines. The people of the Americas knew about and were using this plant well before Europeans, who only discovered it in the late 16th century. Beautiful maps and objects such as Sioux peace-pipes and Cameroon pipes illustrate those early rituals. Before long, tobacco became much sought-after, be it for snuff or smoking in pipes, cigars or cigarettes. Superb collections of tobacco jars, snuff-boxes, pipes made of wood, china and porcelain, clay, meerschaum, glass and deer-horn show the extent of the craze enjoyed by this product, at once medicinal and pleasure-giving – and more recently something that engenders health fears in many people. For Charles Harnisch, a master craftsman and pipe-maker in Colmar in the late 19th century, the creation of a very accurate miniature model of his workshop was intended to promote a then thriving trade. And Dalloz' machine, capable of carving – by copying from an original – a series of several briar pipe-bowls, is a prime example of the technological ingeniousness often shown by these

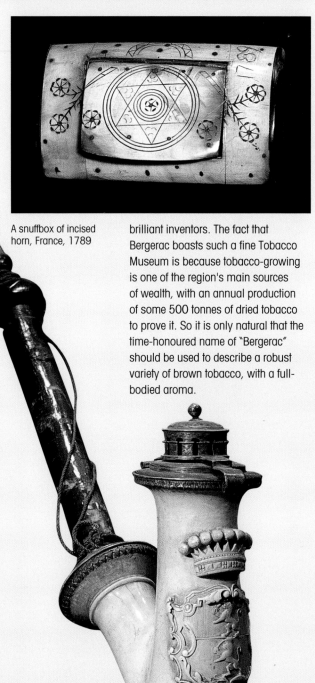

A snuffbox of incised horn, France, 1789

brilliant inventors. The fact that Bergerac boasts such a fine Tobacco Museum is because tobacco-growing is one of the region's main sources of wealth, with an annual production of some 500 tonnes of dried tobacco to prove it. So it is only natural that the time-honoured name of "Bergerac" should be used to describe a robust variety of brown tobacco, with a full-bodied aroma.

Meerschaum pipe, Hungary, 19th century

Monbazillac

Monbazillac castle is a small, harmonious building set on the rolling brow of a hillside down which unfurl wave upon wave of neat, luxuriant vines.It was built by François d'Aydie in 1550 or thereabouts, a pivotal moment between two periods each marked by different architectural concerns. In its layout and in certain of its features, it retains the enclosed aspect of a medieval stronghold with its defensive systems, yet it also includes the embellishment of a Renaissance edifice. It was spared those fearful ravages of history, the Wars of Religion and the French Revolution, surviving intact to offer us both a distinct architectural ensemble and an example of well-balanced decoration, whence a building of great purity. The castle is encircled by a dry moat, crossed by two-arched bridge. A main lodge, flanked by four round, symmetrical pepper-pot towers, lends the structure a solid harmony, heightened by the fringe-like battlement walk running round the top of the castle, itself enhanced by the geometric frieze of its machicolations. The roofs and windows are associated more with a leisurely life-style. The large mullioned windows enliven the façade, which is surmounted by an apparent jumble of timber-work, further complicated by dormer windows and chimneys. The brown and rust-red tiles form an elegant contrast with the grey stone of the lofty walls with wide mullioned windows.

This noble castle stands as a fine symbol for the famed vineyards that bear its name. The Monbazillac Cooperative Winery owns the castle and has helped with the restoration of the building by historian and archaeologist Jean Secret. Several rooms are open to visitors. They house the Protestant Museum, displaying popular arts and crafts, and Perigord furniture. The basement wine-cellars, custodian to various fine Monbazillac vintages, have been turned into a Wine Museum, with an interesting collection of ancient implements.

The wine of Monbazillac

In its shapely bottle, the white wine of Monbazillac is a treat to behold. Golden and heady, when you pour it, it creates gentle waves releasing a subtle "toasty" aroma, with a hint of honey too. The vineyards cover some 6.000 acres, where the main varieties of white grapes grown are sémillon, muscadet and sauvignon. The harvest comes late and involves the tireless task of sorting, where each grape is selected one by one, based on the degree of ripeness, itself the amazing outcome of a secret alchemy at work in each grape affected by botrytis or "noble rot". The morning mists shrouding these hillsides stimulate the growth of a tiny fungus, whose microscopic proliferation is encouraged by the warmth of sunny afternoons. Monbazillac is a stable wine that ages remarkably well. Yes, hard though it may be, this golden treasure is best "forgotten about" for a while, to be rediscovered after several years, sweeter and mellower than ever: a loyal companion to the famous *foie gras* of Perigord.

A bottle of Monbazillac wine

Lanquais, Couze and Lalinde

Lanquais castle, like many Perigord castles, is a composite structure, influenced by the art and architecture of different periods. These overlay one another, but do not affect the harmonious end result. The medieval design included the present-day towers. But in due course this medieval foundation received a Renaissance graft. On the west side, its windows giving on to tranquil gardens clearly date back to this period. The roof is punctuated with dormer windows. The Lanquais chimneys are massive and decorated with elaborate stone tracery. The end result is one of great beauty, but it still awaits completion. One wing, planned to complete a right-angle, was never built. Possession of the family of Isabeau of Limeuil obeying the Catholic Catherine de Medici even to dishonour, the castle's walls still carry the deep wounds left by the religious clashes of the 16th century that pitted Catholic against Protestant in merciless combat.

On the banks of the river Couze, there are a dozen paper mills, some dating back to the 16th century. Before 1700, master paper-makers here manufactured paper with a watermark showing the coat of arms of Amsterdam. In fact, the United Provinces were greedy consumers of paper, because they specialized in publishing printed books. Rouzique mill has been restored, and now brings back to life that age-old activity within an outstanding architectural setting. The old chimneys spring skyward from a maze of buildings erected on the bank where the swift waters of the Couze doggedly batter the paddles of the millwheels. And La Roque mill once again manufactures watermarked paper using time-honoured methods.

Close to the bridge that bestrides the Dordogne at Lalinde, a series of rocks breaks through the surface, forming the hazardous La Gratusse falls, much feared by erstwhile bargemen on the Dordogne.

Catherine de' Medici's "Flying Squad"

As Henri II's widow, regent or advisor to her sons François II, Charles IX and Henri III, from 1559 to 1589, Catherine de' Medici had to govern a kingdom torn apart by the Wars of Religion. An exemplary mother, prepared to do anything to save her children's heritage, she was politically shrewd and keenly aware of the challenge posed to the kingdom of France by the minority of her son, Charles IX who became king in 1560 at the age of ten. But she was also an unscrupulous woman, manoeuvring her way through the intrigues of the French court and never hesitating to choose between negociation and the occult sciences, some even say poison. Sometimes she found human feelings were useful to achieve her political aims. Dressed in window's weeds, she surrounded herself with the pretty young ladies of the nobility to create her "flying squad". The mission of these ladies was to seduce grand princes, make them besotted with love, and thus render them politically innocuous. But in their seductions they were not to fall into love's snare. Isabeau, the "sweet Limeuil", lived in Lanquais, and was a member of these charming battalions. Earmarked to seduce the Prince of Condé, head of the Protestant Party, she succumbed to his charms, and it was soon evident that she was growing plumper beneath her fine silk dresses. Young Isabeau gave birth in secret, in 1564, but not secretly enough to quash the scandal. After a few months spent in a convent, she withdrew to Lanquais where Catherine had her married to the Florentine banker Scipion Sardini who was more than happy to make such a good catch.

Trémolat

Between Badefols-sur-Dordogne and Limeuil, in the crook of a meander of the Dordogne River, Trémolat is dominated by the imposing mass of its fortified church. This is the alleged birthplace of Saint Cybard in the 6th century, and the site of a priory at the end of the 10th, although its foundation by monks from Saint Cybard Abbey in Angoulême certainly took place earlier. The church, the former priory, was built in several stages in the shape of an elongated Latin cross. Given the absence of a fortress, the church's thick, high walls and its massive steeple, like a keep, made it a shelter for clerics as well as the whole population of the village during the troubles of the Hundred Years War and the Wars of Religion. The besieged took refuge in the strong-rooms set above the nave, the choir and the transept and in the steeple. Through the loopholes they could drop projectiles onto the attackers. The bright colours of the stone, with all the shades of ochre and yellow, offset the austere appearance of the church. The three bays in the nave section dating from the 11th century are topped with domes on pendentives, in the tradition of Perigord Romanesque architecture. Another dome covers the transept crossing, which dates from the 12th century, like the choir.

In the cemetery, the tiny Romanesque Saint Hilaire Church features above its door a projecting cornice resting on fine modillions.

But the village is also famous for the unrivalled outlook it offers from the Rocamadou Belvedere arranged north of the village over one of the Dordogne River's most beautiful bends, the Trémolat Meander. The white cliffs looming out of the green vegetation encircle the narrow bend in the river and the two bridges crossing it.

Trémolat: the church of Saint Hilaire

3

FROM THE DORDOGNE TO THE SARLAT AREA

Cadouin

In 1115, several hermits, disciples of Geraud of Sales, gathered at Cadouin, in a remote valley of Bessède Forest. In 1119, the hermitage was affiliated to the Cistercian Order and placed under the authority of the abbot of Pontigny. The monks began work on the abbey church, which was consecrated in 1154, and where they placed the precious relic of the Holy Shroud, perhaps donated by crusaders returning from Antioch. A famous pilgrimage centre, Cadouin developed and prospered. But during the Hundred Years War, the cloister was destroyed and the monks placed the shroud in Toulouse for safe-keeping. After the victory of Castillon in 1453, the shroud was returned to Cadouin where a new cloister in Flamboyant Gothic style was built during the abbacy of Pierre de Gaing. The commendam system and the fighting of the Wars of Religion soon affected community life, which nonetheless resisted and joined the Strict Observance in 1643. However, at the Revolution, the buildings were looted and the archives burned. The monastery was purchased by the mayor of the village and the church became a parish church, probably saving it from destruction. Restored during the 19th and 20th centuries by experts from the Historical Monument Association, today the abbey belongs to the township and the department. As for the Holy Shroud, an evaluation carried out in 1933 on the precious material showed that it dated from the 11th century. Embroidered on the weft, a Kufic inscription evokes an emir called Musta Ali and gives thanks to Allah. Pilgrimages ceased immediately, but the beautiful Fatimid material is still displayed in the abbey's chapterhouse.

The Holy Shroud

When Simon de Montfort, the leader of the Albigensian crusade, made reference, in 1214, to a relic that was in safe-keeping at Cadouin, the scene was set to turn a piece of embroidered linen, brought back from Antioch during those other crusades to the Holy Land, into the authentic shroud that had covered Christ's head. The relic was venerated by many eminent people in France and England alike: Eleanor of Aquitaine, Richard the Lionheart and Saint Louis, to mention just the most famous. The subsequent desire to decipher the strange inscriptions on the cloth and the reservations of historians finally gave rise to considerable doubts. An enquiry was ordered in 1933, and further research was carried out in 1982. When the verdict came, it was cruel and harsh. The cloth was not one of Christ's shrouds. More ironic still, it bears Moslem inscriptions that date from the 11th century, and give thanks to... Allah!

Cadouin: the Holy Shroud

Cadouin church was consecrated in 1154. Its façade is decorated with a row of blind arches and opens through a semi-circular doorway. It has a nave with side aisles, a transept serving two semi-circular chapels and a choir ending with an apse. The nave and side aisles are vaulted with lancet arches and the transept crossing is topped with a dome on pendentives. Five windows set in the wall of the apse illuminate the altar. The steeple with its pyramid-shaped roof rises above the transept crossing. At the end of the 15th century, after the destruction of the Hundred Years War, the cloister was rebuilt in Flamboyant Gothic style but using the walls of the ruined Romanesque cloister. The sculpted capitals in the galleries illustrate biblical parables. Standing against a cloister wall, the abbot's chair is framed with two high-relief friezes depicting the ascent to Mount Calvary and a procession of monks. The back of the chair is carved with the abbey's coat of arms. A long vaulted room that was the abbey's store-room lies in the lay brothers' wing.

Cadouin Abbey: the Abbot's Chair

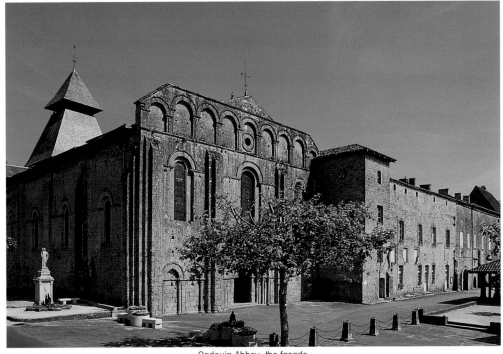

Cadouin Abbey: the façade

Urval and Belvès

Like other Perigord villages, such as Trémolat or Paunat, to mention only those located near the Dordogne-Vézère confluence, Urval has a Romanesque fortified church. It has the same characteristic oblong nave as those in the neighbouring villages. In case of danger, the inhabitants took shelter in the strong-rooms located above the choir dating from the 11th century and those built into the nave during the 12th century. The steeple-wall and the chevet were also built with defence in mind. The only decorative exceptions are the anachronistic voussoirs over the doorway which opens in the western wall. A communal oven has been preserved close to the church.

Above the Nauze River valley, a rocky promontory of sheer cliffs peppered with numerous troglodytic shelters provided protection for a small medieval town, as well as a beautiful view over the area, hence the name Belvès. The town has retained the compact layout of the original medieval *castrum*, with a boulevard where the old town walls once stood. The streets are lined with old houses, their roofs embellished with turrets and pinnacles; several Gothic and Renaissance residences still stand, such as the Archbishop's house. The covered market in the Place d'Armes dates from the 15th century, as does the ancient belfry. Its stout timbers are held up by twenty-three stone pillars. A pillory chain is on display on one of them. The former 14th century Dominican, or Preaching Friars, convent lies on the Place de la Croix-des-Frères.

Some of the troglodytic caves have been restored. In one of the excavations, the mantel of an old fireplace still shows dark traces left by fires. Pottery stands on little wooden shelves and a rustic but functional living-room seems to have been abandoned just a few days earlier.

The right of *Ban*

During the 10th century, the weakness of the Carolingian monarchy provoked the establishment of the right of Ban. The master of the communal seigneury had the right to punish and to order all *manants*, or peasants (from the latin word *manere*, meaning to live, to reside) that is to say all those residing on land subect to his authority. First and foremost, it represented an imposing judicial power. The expeditious procedures of the seigneurial court most often led the accused to the gallows or to pillory. The lord's protection also entailed his right to exact a purely economic ban from the *manants*. He would oblige them to use his communal mill, communal oven and communal press house and would demand, in return, the payment of "banalities", heavy taxes exacted by his cohort of *ministeriales*, his stewards ever keen on profit.

Urval: the communal oven

Les Milandes

In the late 15th century, the Caumont family relegated their mighty martial stronghold at Castelnaud to the rank of garrison and built Milandes Castle, which has all the grace of the finest of Renaissance buildings. In addition to its three large towers, the castle is topped by a sloping roof, where pinnacle turrets, ridge ornaments and dormer windows call to mind the castles of the Loire. No longer needing to protect itself behind a maze of stonework, the castle has an open aspect, turned towards its sweeping terraces with their pierced balustrades. The small castle chapel nearby is in the Flamboyant Gothic style with a side door surmounted by a sculpted Renaissance tympanum. It became a Protestant church when the Lords of Caumont were converted to the Reformed Church. The gardens run down to the Dordogne in gentle terraces, today forming the unique setting for a birds of prey show.

Milandes Castle: a bird of prey

Funny girl

All her life, Josephine Baker (1906-1975) was animated by an exemplary determination and courage which she expressed as much in the glitter of the music hall as in her ideal of universal brotherhood. After having experienced the living conditions of blacks in the American South, Josephine left her native Saint Louis to join a troop of "girls" at the age of thirteen. With her wry expressions, the funny girl was quickly noticed and at the age of sixteen she was already on Broadway. In 1925, she crossed the Atlantic with *La Revue Nègre,* followed by the *Folies Bergères,* where she appeared wearing her famous belt of bananas. Between scandal and triumph, the black Venus conquered Paris and adopted France, her "second love" as the song by Scotto goes. After fighting for her new country during World War II, and once peace had returned, she and her husband, the conductor Jo Bouillon, purchased Milandes castle. There, she installed her "rainbow tribe", the twelve children of all origins whom she adopted, proving to all that "there is only one race, the human race". A terrible manager, Josephine fell into debt and could not prevent the sale of Milandes castle in 1968. In 1975 she had her revenge on Paris, which had turned its back on her, when half a century after the Revue Nègre she triumphed at Bobino just before passing away with this last success.

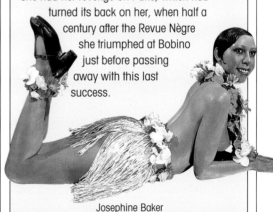

Josephine Baker

Castelnaud

It was in the 12th century that the Cazenac family built a new castle – *castlenaud* – on a promontory on the left bank of the Dordogne, downstream of its confluence with the Céou. In 1214, Simon de Montfort, leader of the Albigensian Crusade found it deserted and installed a garrison. The castle's fate seemed settled by the Treaty of Paris, signed in 1259 by Louis IX and Henry III of England. Quercy, Limousin and Perigord were confirmed as possessions of the Duke of Aquitaine, the king of England in person, and Castelnaud became an English fortress. But the Franco-English conflict revived in 1337, a prologue to the Hundred Years War. The castle faced Beynac, taken by the French in 1368, the year of the marriage between Nompar de Caumont and Magne, the sole heiress of Castelnaud. The French wanted Castelnaud, but they needed time to obtain it. Charles VII worked at it and the fall of Castelnaud in 1442 was a foretaste of his victory in Castillon in 1453. However, the Caumonts retained their privileges and kept their castle. In 1489, François de Caumont undertook the construction of Milandes Castle as his dwelling place. During the Wars of Religion, Castelnaud was occupied by the Huguenot captain Geoffroy de Vivans, a local man. And on May 14, 1610, his lord, Jacques Nompar de Caumont, was in the carriage of his friend King Henri IV the day the king was assassinated by Ravaillac.

Strengthened in the 14th century, Castelnaud had an imposing appearance and all the characteristics of the ideal fortress: the outer walls encircled the bailey, overlooked by curtains and a massive, square keep with machicolations. There is a magnificent panorama of the peaceful Dordogne River valley. A symbol of medieval conflict, Castelnaud is a perfect location for the collections of the Museum of War in the Middle Ages.

The Medieval War Museum

Once the stage of medieval military clashes, the castle of Castlenaud has been a museum of War in the Middle Ages since 1985. A restoration campaign launched in 1996 created new rooms for the exhibition of one hundred and fifty museum pieces from the exceptional Mieg de Boofzheim collection, which enrichened an original collection of one hundred and twenty weapons. Concentrating on defensive and offensive weaponry from the 15th to the 17th centuries, the museum's collections combine the genius of arms manufacturers with the art of goldsmiths. Through swords, shafted weapons, crossbows, artillery, helmets and firearms, the visitor can gain a better understanding of progress in technology, observe typological evolutions, or take in a few spectacular pieces such as the 16th century organ formed of twelve canons. War machines are exhibited outside: the trebucket, which could project a cannonball weighing fifty kilograms two hundred metres away; the *bricole*, whose effectiveness had nothing to do with the "odds and ends" its name evokes, and the bombard, the canon's ancestor. During the summer, there are even demonstrations allowing visitors to discover how these war machines used to work.

A battle-axe, 15th century

Marqueyssac

Between Beynac and La Roque-Gageac, Marqueyssac is situated on a rocky promontory dominating the Dordogne River, opposite the feudal castle of Castelnaud which is set on the other bank. Built, for the most part, at the end of the 18th century or the beginning of the 19th century, a round tower at its centre serves as the only reminder of the 15th century construction which preceded it. Tradition has it that it was one of Le Notre's best students, a certain Mr. Porcher, who designed the first plans for the park commissioned by Bertrand Vernet, the owner of the estate in 1692. It was in 1861 that Julien de Cerval, a judge from Sarlat, acquired Marqueyssac, transforming it into one of Perigord's most beautiful parks. As a volunteer in the Roman legion of pontifical guards, this lover of botany derived inspiration from the gardens of an Italy he had come to know well. The park spreads out over twenty-two hectares. To the west, where the terraces and the bastion meet the evenly laid out flower beds and more private gardens, Julien de Cerval built a neo-medieval chapel along with an Italian inspired loggia. Beginning at the path lined with rosemary bushes to the east, three walks and a total of six kilometres of winding paths cover an area fitted up with rock work, grottos, waterfalls, steps, a labyrinth and theatres of greenery. An estimated 150.000 box trees frame the flower beds and alleyways. Only their curved rows seem to contain the overflowing vegetation made up of cypress trees, yuccas, junipers, umbrella pines, evergreen oaks, or Montpellier maples. Mediterranean type vegetation does well in the dry, limestone earth on the southern side of the promontory, while to the north grow trees from the Atlantic climate such as the hornbeam or the robinia. The contrast is striking when witnessed from the belvedere. In this green expanse a panorama of exceptional sites are also waiting to be discovered in the valley of the Dordogne River, from Domme to Beynac.

Marqueyssac: the castle

◀ A view of the Dordogne River and La Roque-Gageac seen from Marqueyssac Gardens

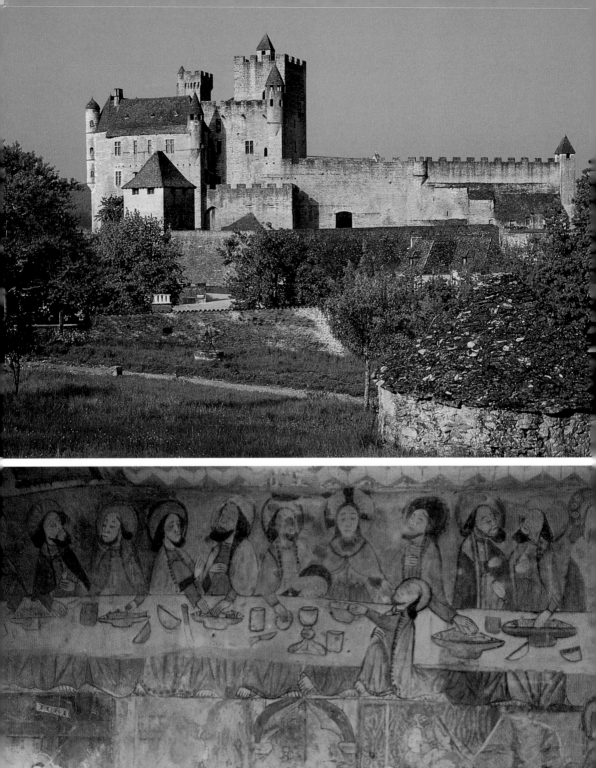

Beynac

Opposite the castle of Castelnaud, Beynac Castle is perched on the summit of a cliff. At its foot, one hundred and fifty metres below, the village houses with their shale roofs spread as far as the right bank of the Dordogne. The old quays are a reminder that the river used to be the scene of intensive river transportation. A very steep footpath, the *Caminal des Panieraires*, leads from the village to the castle. During the Middle Ages, Beynac was one of the four baronies of Perigord. Adhemar of Beynac took part in the Second Crusade in 1147. In 1152, Louis VII repudiated Eleanor of Aquitaine, who married Henry Plantagenet in 1152 and brought Aquitaine as her dowry. When Henry became King of England as Henry II two years later, his possessions on French territory, including the Duchy of Normandy and the County of Anjou, were greater than those of the king of France, whose vassal he was for those three fiefs. In 1194, the inevitable war broke out between Philip Augustus, the son of Louis VII, and Richard the Lionheart, the son of Henry II and Eleanor, who occupied Beynac. When the lord of Beynac refused his ultimatum in 1214, Simon de Montfort had the keep and castle ramparts destroyed. And during the Hundred Years War, Beynac, which had been English since the Treaty of Paris in 1259, returned to French hands in 1368. The castle was rebuilt during the 13th century, and the main building was added in the 14th. In the latter, the Hall of the States of Perigord, with its ribbed vaulting, contains a Renaissance fireplace. The oratory is decorated with frescos showing Jesus at the foot of the Cross, Saint Christopher, as well as the Last Supper at which Saint Martial is serving a dish. A 17th century staircase leads to the covered way, which offers a vast panorama of the Dordogne River valley with the castles of Fayrac, Castelnaud and Marqueyssac. In the distance, the Barre de Domme is just visible.

The Archeological Park

The Archeological Park of Beynac offers a hands-on approach to daily life during the period ranging from the Neolithic to the Roman conquest, from 6.000 to 52 B.C., at the very foundation of peasant society. As a symbol of the timelessness of man's presence on the land, the museum was installed in the tower of a medieval castle built on a late Bronze Age dwelling, back when a village had developed on these heights above the Dordogne valley during the 8th to the 7th century B.C. While the exhibition rooms present objects of Neolithic and protohistoric culture along with their new technologies such as pottery, weaving or metal casting, the Archeological Park, set at the foot of the castle, has a life-sized approach to these ancient times. An entire village behind a fortified Roman door brings the activities of the Neolithic, the Bronze Age and the Iron Age back to life. With the help of experimental archeology, our settled ancestors' houses were built in the village out of wood and cob while workshops demonstrate the techniques of weaving, flint-cutting or the firing of ceramics. A Neolithic dolmen, a Bronze Age temple and a Gallic tree are there to evoke the religious beliefs of these changing societies.

A granary

La Roque-Gageac

At the foot of a towering cliff hewn out by the Dordogne, the small walled village of La Roque-Gageac offers an array of white and ochre façades. The village is strung out like a pretty pearl necklace, wedged between the narrow river bank and the sheer rock face behind. On the house façades, the neatly dressed stones come in every shade of ochre, and the perfect harmony thus created calls to mind some ideal stage set. Dovetailed one into the next, the houses seem to be besieging the cliff. Downstream, the Dordogne grows still and calm. Its waters, smooth like a fathomless mirror, create a double image by reflecting the walled village upside down. It is worth clambering up the narrow lanes that cling close to the rock. The stroll becomes quite spell-binding when an astonishing tropical garden suddenly appears, growing along a narrow ledge in the cliff. Palm trees, bananas, agave, fig trees, cacti and bamboo all thrive here, revelling in the warm sun's rays bouncing off the rock. You will instantly think you are in other, distant climes, for this is a region where chestnut, poplar and walnut hold sway. You can walk further on to the troglodytic forts, impressive man-made structures, cleverly fashioned from natural hollows in the rock.

The manor belonging to the Tarde family is a stately Renaissance building with a round tower and mullioned windows. Jean Tarde (1561-1636) was canon of La Roque-Gageac. What a mind! Like his colleague Pico della Mirandola, he was a "bottomless fount of knowledge". Astronomer and geographer, archaeologist and historian, mathematician and physician, theologian and philosopher, he was driven by a tireless curiosity and passion for everything. Indeed, his aim was to master all the knowledge of his day!

Just downstream from the village, La Malartrie castle is a good example of a 19th century edifice constructed in the Renaissance style.

La Roque-Gageac

Domme

The exceptional location offered by the rocky promontory called the Barre de Domme, overlooking the meanders of the Dordogne, was occupied in the 12th century by a fortress that was captured by Simon de Montfort in 1214, during his campaign in Perigord. The military chief of the Albigensian Crusade had the keep – "very high, very beautiful and mortared nearly to the top" – dismantled, according to Guy des Vaux-de-Cernay, an eyewitness to the events and chronicler of the crusade. The site's strategic importance was not ignored by Philip the Bold who, in 1281, ordered his seneschal to found a bastide there. In 1283, a customary charter was granted to the inhabitants. The English were not far away and Domme had to be defended. On the cliff side, the cliff itself was sufficiently dissuasive, but ramparts were built on the three other sides. They are similar to those in Aigues-Mortes. The walls contain three gates: Bos Gate, Combe Gate and Tower Gate. In the west, the Bos Gate with its pointed arch was reinforced with a large portcullis. In the south, the Combe Gate is much smaller and has a simple archway at the foot of the ramparts. In the east, the last and most imposing, Tower Gate, opens onto the Place d'Armes. It is best admired from outside the walls on the road to Groléjac. The two semi-circular towers with bosses framing the Gothic-arched opening were used as guard rooms but also as prisons for the Templar Knights incarcerated there from 1307 to 1318. Evidence is seen in the signs and drawings engraved in the stone. On the cliff side, the bastide willed by Philip the Bold has retained the characteristic layout of these new towns but the checkerboard plan changes as soon as one moves further away. The Place de la Halle (Market Square) is the heart of the town. Pillars of pale stone hold up the massive timber frame with sloping roofs of the recently restored covered market. Just op-

Knights of Christ

In 1118, during the first Crusade, a group of crusaders led by Hugues de Payns founded the brotherhood of the Poor Knights of Christ. Saint Bernard defined its rule in 1133: "The knight of Christ causes death in complete security and receives it with even more assurance. If he dies, it is for his own good; if he kills, it is for the good of Christ." Badouin II provided his residence in Jerusalem, the former mosque al-Aqsa, known as "the Temple". Well organized, well armed, and well fed – it was not recommended to abstain from eating meat for it weakened the body– the Order of the Temple inspired vocations and donations. The knights wore a white mantle with a red cross atop their armour complete with helmut, coat of mail, lance, shield and sword. They made a vow of poverty, of chastity and obedience and any breach of this vow led to the "loss of the House", meaning expulsion. The Order acquired wealth but the end of the Frankish States of the Holy Land signed its own end. In a trial instigated by Philip the Fair, they were accused of corruption of morals, heresy and collusion with Infidels. Arrested on October 13th, 1307 and subjected to torture, the Templars confessed, then withdrew their confession and were burned at the stake in 1314 with the Grand Master of the order, Jacques de Molay.

Domme, Tower Gate: Templar graffiti

posite, the Governors' House, seat of the tourist office, is a fine building with a regular façade, flanked with a tall pepper-pot tower. Near the Bos Gate, the Place de la Rode hides a cruel history behind its name. Rode was the French term for the wheel. The condemned person was drawn and quartered, beaten, and had his arms and legs broken and torn off. The houses surrounding the square have been well renovated, like the one belonging to Philip the Bold's money minter with its trifoiled windows.

Caves, whose access is near the market, contain interesting concretions. But it was not to admire the beauty of the stalactites that the inhabitants of Domme took refuge there, but to escape the violence of the Hundred Years War and the Wars of Religion. During the latter, Captain Geoffroy de Vivans, a fierce Protestant, had tried to enter the stronghold twice. His two failed attempts increased his determination to succeed. One evening in October 1588, with about thirty men, he set about scal-

ing the only unguarded access – the Barre de Domme. He reached the summit in complete silence, having spread blankets on the ground to muffle the noise. The town was asleep. The captain decided to rouse it with loud hate-filled cries and warring noises. He captured the town, established a garrison and occupied it for four years, managing to impose the re-formed faith on its inhabitants. He burned down the church as well as the priory of Cénac. Joining forces with the Catholics, he left the town for a payment of forty thousand *livres* after dismantling it.

Only the Romanesque chevet of Cénac priory survived the fire lit by Geoffroy de Vivans. This priory had been founded at the end of the 12th century on lands acquired by Aquilanus, Abbot of Moissac. The church contains about thirty sculpted capitals mainly depicting plant and animal motifs, but also historiated capitals like those showing Daniel in the lions' den or the resurrection of Lazarus.

Domme, Tower Gate: a loophole

Cénac: the chevet of the church

Domme: the covered market and the Governor's Mansion ▶

Fénelon

Between the Quercy region of Bouriane and the Dordogne, two castles round out the list of the Perigourdian heritage " land of a thousand and one castles". But could there really be only a thousand? 17th century Veyrignac castle, destroyed during World War II, has since been restored. At the top of a hillock stands Fénelon castle with its august towers. It looks down on a small village bearing a mild, though legendary name: Saint Mondane, mother of Saint Sacerdos, bishop of Limoges and patron saint of the town of Sarlat. Mondane was living the life of a recluse in a cave, when the Saracen invasion of Aquitaine forced her to join in the fight against the Infidel. She perished in the act, and was buried in her cave dwelling. Subsequently, a surge of fervour and devotion has brought a mass of pilgrims to these parts, attracted by the growing number of miracles worked by the saint.

Set solid and haughty on the lowest terraces of the Dordogne valley, the castle property of the Salignac-Fénelon has retained a beautiful cohesion, despite successive additions from the 15th to 17th centuries. It harmoniously combines the severity of a medieval fortress, on the one hand, with its triple walls, its large corner towers hemmed with machicolations, and the parapet walk between the alternating crenellations and battlements, and, on the other, all the gentle elegance of a Renaissance dwelling, where comfort and ornament are more important than effective defences. Mullioned windows, dormer windows with carvings of heraldic trophies, tall chimneys, balustraded galleries and terraces, all enliven the aspect and lend this castle a fairy-tale quality. The magnificent roof is covered with *lauzes*, those usually undressed, heavy slabs of limestone. Only hale and solid chestnut wood could bear the weight as it increases, row by row, to the top of the frame. A room houses a collection of objects and furniture which belonged to Fénelon.

His name is Fénelon – for short

François de Salignac de La Mothe Fénelon, son of Pons de Salignac de La Mothe Fénelon and Louise de La Cropte Chantérac, was born on August 6, 1651 in this splendid Fénelon Castle. By a shortcut which comes close to being irreverent, we know him by the name of Fénelon, the great writer of the age of Louis XIV. He belonged to the upper echelons of the provincial nobility. His *Telemachus* is a collection of writings on the ideal upbringing of a prince. Indeed, he dedicated it to the Duke of Burgundy, grandson of Louis XIV, who was earmarked as the probable heir to the French crown, had he not died before his robust grandfather. Fénelon was duly appointed Archbishop of Cambrai, where he defended certain profoundly mystical concepts and took violent issue with another great thinker of the day, Bossuet.

In disgrace, and exiled on account of his somewhat overly novel ideas, Fénelon died at Cambrai in 1715, a good way from his native Perigord.

Bust of Fénelon

Montfort

The Montfort Loop is, with that of Trémolat, one of the most famous meanders in the Dordogne valley. A belvedere set on the cliff lets the visitor appreciate the river's course, carved out over thousands of years. The outer bank, sheer and tall, receives the full force of the river's impetuous surge, assailing it head on and laying bare the deep layers of white limestone. But the land resists the onslaught and the river, forced to change direction, describes an almost perfect arc of a circle. The opposite, inner bank is low-lying and stony. On the rocky promontory overlooking the loop, Montfort Castle occupies a choice strategic vantage point, which has brought it its share of trials and tribulations over the centuries. In 1214, the castle, abandoned by its lord Bertrand de Cazenac, was destroyed by Simon de Montfort but "the walls were so solid that they were difficult to demolish", recounts Guy des Vaux-de-Cernay in his *Historia Albigensis*. If this chronicler were to be believed, Bertrand de Cazenac and his wife, the sister of the Viscount of Turenne, were rather unsavoury characters. They robbed pilgrims and destroyed churches. Montfort's crusaders even discovered a hundred and fifty men and women who had taken refuge in the Benedictine abbey in Sarlat. They had been atrociously mutilated by the infernal couple; some had had their hands or feet cut off, their eyes torn out, or their breasts ripped off. Montfort Castle, a fief of the Turennes, was rebuilt then destroyed under Louis XI and Henry IV, but each time it rose again from its ashes. Although the left wing was restored in the 19th century, the remaining sections are reconstructions from the 15th and 16th centuries.

On the other side of the loop, upstream from the castle, on the shores of the Enea, a tributary of the Dordogne, Carsac has a Romanesque church. Inside, the stained glass windows are modern, the Way of the Cross was made by Zack, and the accompanying texts are taken from the work of Paul Claudel.

Carsac: the church

Sarlat

Sarlat lies in the heart of a wooded valley of Black Perigord. With its heart-shaped layout, once bounded by defensive walls, the town bursts with colour, from the pale limestone of its buildings to the sombre greys of its roofs, standing out starkly against the surrounding greenery. Sarlat is a remarkable town that was able to preserve or restore its architectural heritage. A stroll through its winding streets whisks the visitor back to the past. A Benedictine abbey was founded in the 830's by Duke Pepin of Aquitaine, who charged the monks holding the relics of St. Sacerdos to protect them from raiding Norsemen, who were laying waste to the area by cleverly using the thoroughfare provided by the Dordogne River. Sarlat Abbey prospered, directing sixty priories, while a first town grew up around it. But the population was regularly decimated by plague epidemics and flooding

Malraux's Law

As a result of this law dealing with renovation and restoration work, Sarlat was assisted by the financial aid needed to safeguard a very rich heritage. The treasure that the Ministry of Culture of the day intended to save included 25 acres, 253 buildings, 14 listed monuments, and 52 registered monuments. The restoration of façades, the bracing of *lauze*-covered roofs, the re-paving of streets, the addition of a certain level of comfort into these ancient dwellings, all have made Sarlat's historic centre a fine example of carefully conceived renovation. Such a subtle compromise was certainly costly, and subsidies and loans compelled the town council and Sarlat's citizenry to feel as one in this undertaking. The outcome is nothing but positive, even if certain boroughs still need protection and improvement.

Sarlat: Saint-Sacerdos Cathedral

◄ Sarlat: Old stone houses

by the Cuze Stream flowing through the town. In 1147, Bernard of Clairvaux travelled through Aquitaine and Languedoc preaching against the heresy spread by Henry of Lausanne. He stopped in Sarlat, praising the theological and rhetorical teaching at St. Sacerdos Abbey. As there was yet another plague epidemic, Bernard prayed and blessed the bread he gave the ill. The epidemic ebbed. The strange Lantern of the Dead, at the end of the Recessed Tombs Garden, may have been raised to commemorate this miracle.

Then the abbot, uncontested lord of the town until the end of the 13th century, had to acknowledge the increasing power of the consuls, notables from the urban elite, jurists, wealthy merchants or troubadours. Power sharing between the abbot and the consuls was confirmed in the Book of Peace in 1299, and immediately influenced the urban landscape of Sarlat with, on one side the monastic enclosure and, on the other, the consular town. When Pope John XXII created the diocese of Sarlat in 1317, St. Sacerdos Abbey Church stood in the heart of a town surrounded by solid ramparts.

Near the borderline between French and English territories, the town suffered greatly from the first clashes of the Hundred Years War and, by the Treaty of Brétigny of 1360, Sarlat had to pledge allegiance to Edward III, King of England. But Sarlat remained French at heart and took an active part in the struggle against the English. It finally gained its freedom, but at a high price. The end of the 15th and the 16th centuries was the high point for the town. Sarlat contained wealthy families of the judicial nobility (noblesse de robe), king's councillors or magistrates, who built fine mansions, such as Plamon, Maleville or Vassal. Sarlat also had a Town Hall where the consuls sat, a Presidial where the central power named the seneschalsy was exercised, convents, hospitals and elegant dwellings, like that belonging to the family of Montaigne's friend de La Boétie, who died of the

Sarlat: the Presidial or royal court of justice

plague in 1563. Along with the latter, other humanists and poets attuned to the new ideas of the Italian Renaissance turned Sarlat into a small intellectual capital throughout the 16th century.

During the same period, the deeply Catholic town was the scene of conflicts of the Wars of Religion. The Protestants, led by Geoffroy de Vivans, captured the town on Carnival Day, 1574, in revenge for the massacres of Saint Barthelemy in 1572. They scattered the relics of St. Sacerdos. At the end of hostilities, Sarlat felt that it had recovered some calm, but it soon plunged once again into the troubles of the Fronde. A stake in a battle far beyond its understanding, Sarlat was invested by Condé between 1652 and 1653. Despite a situation judged hardly favourable for development by the Intendant of Guyenne, Bazin de Bezons, who in 1698 described it as, "…it is in a depth surrounded by mountains; there is no river", the town prospered discreetly, perhaps a bit too discreetly, since it was eventually forgotten in the heart of sleepy Perigord. The fever pitch of the 19th century Industrial Revolution barely reached it even though it was during that century that the Rue de la République, called the Traverse, was planned. This commercial street divides the town into two sections. And even the construction of the railway did not manage to stir Sarlat from its docile lethargy. This may have been just as well, for it allowed the town to preserve an architectural heritage which it has been emphasizing ever since.

On the Place du Peyrou, adjacent to the bishop's palace, Saint Sacerdos Cathedral is a building whose complexity results from the abbey's eventful history, and then, from 1317 to 1790, the history of the Sarlat bishopric whose seat was occupied by members of the Salignac-Fénelon Family from 1567 to 1639 and from 1659 to 1688. From its Romanesque founding, it has retained its belfry-porch and its façade with three blind arches. The elevation of the nave walls, supported by solid fly-

Étienne de La Boétie

É tienne de La Boétie was born in 1530 in Sarlat, into a family of the Perigord bourgeoisie connected to the magistracy. After studying classics at Guyenne College in Bordeaux, where Michel de Montaigne was also a pupil, La Boétie went to study law at the University of Orleans. He was a brilliant student and after obtaining his diploma, he was named councillor to the Bordeaux Parliament in 1553, two years before the required legal age. When Michel de Montaigne, three years younger, also became a councillor in 1557, the two men became close friends. On the eve of the Wars of Religion, La Boétie, linked to the Chancellor Michel de l'Hospital, distinguished himself by his moderate opinions, trying to implement tolerant policies at the Bordeaux Parliament, which was inclined to be repressive. In 1562, his *Essay on the Edict of January (Mémoire sur l'Édit de Janvier)* was opposed to fanatical Catholics as well as Protestants. But the following year, a plague epidemic in Sarlat during the summer brought about La Boétie's premature death at the age of 33. Montaigne, "his intimate brother and sacred friend", inherited his books and manuscripts and undertook their publication. A poet, La Boétie left behind *Twenty-Nine Amorous Sonnets,* written when he was 16-17, that Montaigne published in Book I of Essays; Latin verse, as well as translations of Xenonphon and Plutarch, published in 1570; French verse, published in 1571. However, Montaigne decided not to publish *Contr'Un,* also called *Discourse of Voluntary Servitude (Discours de la servitude volontaire),* written by La Boétie at the age of 18. Extolling the freedom inherent in everyone, against tyranny, "be resolved to serve no longer and you will be free", this text was rapidly considered to be an anti-monarchical pamphlet and was used by Protestants in 1574, and was reprinted during each period of struggle for democracy, most notably in 1789.

ing buttresses, is in Gothic style, as are the small chapels opening onto the side aisles. The onion-shaped roof of the bell-tower was built later and shows classical influences. This disparity and mixture of styles, periods and manners make this quite a particular building. The interior likewise lacks unity but displays furnishings that are at once composite but extremely opulent, like the 18th century organ loft, a masterpiece of the famous Clicquot family, organ-makers in Reims. A maze of small courtyards, stairways, terraces and narrow passages provides access to a courtyard where the former cloister used to stand to the south of the cathedral. Only three arcades remain. The same courtyard is the setting for the Chapel of the Blue Penitents, the former Saint Benedict's Chapel from the 12th century. It is sober and elegant like all Romanesque buildings, evidence of the bygone splendour of Sarlat Abbey. In the Fountain Courtyard, clear water springing forth from three small channels explains the monks' original settlement in this place. The nearby Canons' Courtyard features a beautiful old house with half-timbered walls and a corbelled construction. Finally, behind the cathedral's chevet, the Garden of the Tomb Recesses is a reminder that monks lived and died here. It is still possible to see the tombs hewn out of the outer wall. A staircase leads to Sarlat's most mysterious building, both in form and function. The Lantern of the Dead is a cylindrical structure topped by a tapered cone-shaped roof. Was it a monument raised to commemorate the miracle of Saint Bernard in 1147, or a lantern of the dead whose flickering light was intended to remind people, on dark nights, of the dreaded, fearsome presence of tombs in the nearby cemetery? One mystery remains. It would seem that access to the upper part of the tower, where the lamp supposedly stood, is particularly awkward if not impassable for adults. How then can we imagine that the lantern was kept permanently fuelled and under surveillance?

A Crusade in Perigord

The heretics that Bernard de Clairvaux tried to return to the straight road of orthodoxy were not Cathares. But the seeds of this dualistic heresy were certainly already present on the Occitanian lands. Several years later, the Albigensian doctrine had spread principally in the Toulouse area but also in Perigord, as related by a monk named Heribert in a chronicle dated 1163. "Numerous heretics arrived in Perigord, claiming to live the apostolic life," he wrote. He continued, "Into this trickery, many people entered, not only nobles, leaving behind their belongings, but also clerics, priests, monks and nuns." In 1208, Pope Innocent launched his appeal for a crusade against the Albigensians. In 1212, while on campaign in the Agenais area, Simon de Montfort captured Biron, held by Martin Algaï. The latter was dragged attached to a horse's tail, before being hanged.

In 1214, Perigord saw the arrival of troops led by Simon de Montfort. In Sarlat, the crusaders discovered one hundred and fifty men and women atrociously mutilated by Bertrand de Cazenac. When the troops arrived under the walls of Domme, Montfort and Castelnaud, the fortresses had already been abandoned, despite their strategic locations and the solidity of their fortifications, described by Pierre des Vaux-de-Cernay in his *Historia Albigensis*. The first two castles were demolished; Castelnaud was spared by de Montfort who installed a garrison there. As for Beynac, the "seat of Satan" for the same chronicler, the fief of a lord who was "very dangerous, a cruel tyrant and a brutal oppressor of the church", its keep was ruined.

Sarlat: the Garden of the Recessed Tombs and the Lantern of the Dead ▶

The Presidial – the erstwhile Royal Court – is one of the town's most arresting buildings. The pale stonework of its façade, with two arches one atop the other, is covered, right to the broad *lauze* roof, with the energetic branches of a luxuriant Virginia creeper. The central lantern turret with its elegant festooned roof is supported by a set of dressed beams which afford a glimpse of a pinnacle turret with stained-glass windows. The light captured by these windows bathes the beautiful stairways in an irreal clarity. The most famous building of all in Sarlat is without doubt La Boétie Mansion, with its elongated façade, and a fine gable decorated with small kale-shaped carvings.

The mullioned windows opening on to the square are all edged with carved string-courses, which reach a crescendo on the topmost floor, with a veritable burst of symmetrically arranged medallions, arabesques and scroll-type foliage motifs. Turrets and pinnacles reach upward, rounding off the intricate and refined decoration, greatly influenced by 16th century Italian art. The town's streets and squares are all lined with noteworthy houses, two of which merit a lingering visit: the rue de la Liberté, with its half-timbered buildings and the magnificent Maleville Mansion, also known as the Vienne Mansion. Built by Jean de Vienne in the 16th century, it became the residence of the de Brons family and was acquired by the Malevilles in the 19th century. Finest of all, the narrow, winding Rue des Consuls, boasting, among an array of fine buildings, the Plamon Mansion, also known as the Consuls' Mansion. It was purchased by Guillaume Plaumon in 1473 and served as residence to this family of consuls until the 17th century. Opposite, the 15th century Vassal Mansion, with its twin-turreted tower is contiguous to the Gisson mansion, from the 16th century. Last of all, the chapel of the White Penitents is a Baroque edifice, its doorway topped by a pediment decorated with volutes. The overly schematic style of our modern buildings has not yet ousted the confusion, profusion and delicate charm of Sarlat's volumes, with their broken lines and odd recesses.

Sarlat: Plamon Mansion

Sarlat: the entrance to the chapel of the White Penitents

Puymartin

On the road from Sarlat to Les-Eyzies-de-Tayac, before reaching the little village of Allas, the slender silhouette of Puymartin Castle stands out against the blue sky. The castle dates from the 15th and 16th centuries, but was restored in the 19th. Inside, it is luxuriously decorated. The great hall with its fine fireplace ornamented with a surprising imitation frame in trompe-l'œil and precious furnishings, contains six Flemish tapestries showing scenes of the Trojan War. The walls in the main bedroom are hung with a set of *verdures*, 18th century Aubusson tapestries. The wainscoting in a study is painted with scenes presenting various mythological themes, such as the *Mysteries of Eleusis* or the legend of the wild boar of Calydon. They are believed to have been painted about 1670 by Philippe Lemaire, an artist from Laon, who settled in Sarlat after his marriage.

Puymartin Castle: the Mythological Chamber

Le Breuil Huts

The dry-stone huts or *bories* in the hamlet of Le Breuil are famous not because they are one of a kind, but rather because of the way they form an impressive grouping of five hut-like structures. They have thick walls made of overlaid limestone blocks which support a roof of flat slabs, the famous *lauzes*. These slabs are arranged in circular layers and are slightly staggered to form a dome, which culminates at the top in a perfect water-tight cone. The unobtrusive contours of the softly rounded roofs, fitting snugly with the round shape of the base and merging with the gentle outlines of the adjoining hut, make this collection of buildings one of unusual charm. The mysterious origins of this stone "architecture of necessity", where the apparent simplicity of the construction conceals a perfect mastery of concepts of equilibrium, weight, mass and divergent forces, are certainly very remote.

Le Breuil Huts

Through Black Perigord

North of Sarlat, Notre Dame Chapel in Temniac contains a Black Virgin which inspired pilgrimages for a long time. Built on a hill overlooking Sarlat, the village was the seat of a Templar Commandery before it became the residence of the Sarlat bishops. This area abounds in manors. They are not quite castles, but sufficiently well-to-do to include features like pepper-pot turrets, pinnacles, and impressive *lauze*-tiled roofs. Eyrignac manor is enhanced by magnificent gardens which were created by Antoine de Costes de Calprenède in the 17th century. The intricate frieze of box bushes pruned in arabesque motifs stands out starkly against a tender green carpet of lawn, subtly hemmed by fine, if daintily dishevelled yews. Nature here is managed, subject to the wishes of a head gardener who is a pastmaster in the art of wielding square and compass, measuring-tape and secateurs.

The original Salignac castle was probably built during the 11th century, but virtually nothing remains of that early stronghold. A massive, square, 12th century keep, surmounted by elegant 18th century timberwork forming four walls, a main building in the most thorough Renaissance tradition, with beautiful, clearly defined windows, large round towers with roofs shaped like flared cones. The castle still belongs to a descendant of the Salignac-Fénelon lineage.

Built on a human scale, Saint-Géniès is the perfect model of a classic Perigord village, with its lovely Romanesque church and houses huddled chaotically about it. Le Cheylard Chapel is a tiny building erected on top of a grassy hillock. It was founded in 1329, to the year, the inscription in Gothic lettering being engraved above the entrance door. Its walls were once covered with beautiful frescoes showing scenes from lives of Christ and the Saints, such as the martyr Saint Catherine. Painted in the Gothic style during the 14th

Temniac: Notre Dame Chapel

century, these murals decorate the vaults and walls, delineated by pointed archways.

La Grande Filolie castle, is worth driving up to, even if you may not visit it. This is truly a legendary manor house, and as you admire the complicated 14th and 15th century architecture, a whole host of beautiful ladies in iridescent robes springs into the mind's eye. It is redolent of both *Grand Meaulnes* castle and *Sleeping Beauty*, and it has everything: tall, ivy-clad towers, broad, *lauze*-slabbed roofs, and mullioned windows with sweeping views over a fresh, green valley. La Cassagne, in the hushed recesses of an age-old valley, huddles about a Romanesque church and its fine 15th century presbytery. The Doux spring is a resurgence. From it flow considerable volumes of water that has seeped into the rock mass of the nearby limestone plateaus, the *causses*. More than four kilometres of its underground course have already been explored by divers. This extremely pure water sparkles with blue and green highlights, and forms the stream called the Coly.

Le Cheylard Chapel: Mural of Saint George

Oil with a native tang

As the leading producer of walnuts in France, Perigord has turned this small, wrinkled fruit into a veritable culture. Its famous oil flavours the products from its native soil and give a little local colour to even the simplest of salads. To make it, the walnut mills use hydraulic power such as the one of la Tour, in Sainte-Nathalène, where the paddle wheels are turned by the river waters of the Enea. Built around the 16th century, it still uses traditional methods and its 19th century machines. After the walnut meats have been removed from their shells, they are ground down by a thirty kilogram millstone which is turned by a paddle wheel. The resulting paste is heated in a cauldron. The amount of oil and its quality depend on true expertise during this critical stage when the perfect temperature must be determined to bring out the flavours, evaporate the water and liquefy the oil. It is then time for pressing the paste, when fifteen litres of natural oil are obtained from the original thirty kilograms of walnuts. After a week's decanting, it is ready to offer all its subtle flavour to Perigordian *cuisine*.

La Tour Mill: the millstone

Saint-Amand-de-Coly

According to legend, a first monastic foundation on the shores of the Coly in the 7th century was due to Saint Amand. In the 12th century Augustinian canons built the priory of Saint Amand, of which the church – fortified to the extent that it was sometimes called Saint Amand Fort – remains. Its first abbot, William, died at the beginning of the 12th century and was buried in the church. A burial inscription to the glory of the deceased is still visible inside the church in the north absidal chapel. The abbey underwent a rapid but brief period of expansion but, by 1347, it contained only seven monks. When the commendam system was inaugurated in the 14th century, the abbey became the de *facto* possession of the Ferrières family, whose members were in charge of the abbey for one hundred and ninety-two years. In 1577, a garrison of Huguenot troops entrenched themselves here, and it took the governor of Perigord, at the head of two thousand horsemen, six days of cannon-fire to overcome their resistance.

Saint-Amand-de-Coly abbey church, both monumental and grandiose, seems out of proportion with the tiny village huddling around it. The sole remaining trace of the priory, the church is built against the rock-face of the hill that encircles the chevet. Access is along a path of uneven and worn flagstones that first passes through an ancient fortified gate. The western facade is impressive with its huge pointed arch framing the doorway and a window. At the top of the arch lies a strong-room with small doors opening in its west, south and north sides.

A dark, narrow passage leads around the church, lined on one side by the building's solid walls and on the other by the damp, sheer rock wall which supports the church's stout buttresses. The corbels framing the walls are further evidence of additional fortifications, long since vanished. The top of the ramparts were undoubtedly once crowned with a covered walk, watchtowers, pepper-pot turrets and wooden walkways. The necessary simplicity of the architecture, reduced to a few voussoirs supported by slender columns, their capitals decorated with leaf motifs, emphasizes the monument's severe austerity. The inside is surprising. The slight gradient already sensed before the entrance to the nave is extended here by a progressive elevation of the floor as far as the raised choir, with its adjacent flat chevet lit by three semicircular arched windows. The very tall nave is bare. The long columns supporting the walls merge in a handsome, impressively sober Gothic vault. The transept is lined with small blind arcades with pointed arches, a slight break with the simplicity of the building. Just a few capitals contrast with the sobriety, one in the south absidal chapel in particular on which two bodies are devoured by a lion and a dragon.

Saint-Amand-de-Coly: nave of the abbey church

4

THE VÉZÈRE VALLEY

Condat-sur-Vézère and Montignac

After feeding a mill, the waters of the Coly River join those of the Vézère at the village of Condat, whose name of Celtic origin means confluence. In the 14th century, a Templar Commandery, which became the property of the Hospitallers of Saint John of Jerusalem after 1312, was founded there. A square 15th century keep, a 16th century dwelling house, a fortified church, rearranged several times, with its charming wall-bell tower, make up the remaining vestiges. Well before the discovery of the cave at Lascaux brought it fame, Montignac, a small town of Black Perigord well located on the right bank of the Vézère River, had a long history behind it. Gallo-Romans succeeded prehistoric occupation of the site. During the 11th century, its fortress – a stronghold whose importance was already attested in the 10th century – became the possession of the Counts of Perigord. Subsequently, it changed owner, passing from the Orléans to the Albrets before Henry IV ceded it to François de Hautefort, Lord of Thenon. Today the castle is only an isolated silhouette on a rocky escarpment, its tower overlooking the Vézère. The writer Eugène Le Roy was born in the town and lived in the narrow streets of old houses in Montignac, and along the riverbanks with their houses on stilts. A museum located in the former Gothic hospital is dedicated to him. It presents the work and daily life of the people of Perigord, described by Le Roy in *Jacquou le Croquant* and other novels. Discovered in 1957 near Lascaux, in a cave where bears hibernated and their bones have been well-preserved, the Régourdou deposit contained the tomb of a young Neanderthal man, from about 70.000 years ago. His skeleton is on display at the Museum of Perigord.

The Gardens of the Imagination

Overlooking the valley of the Vézère River, the Gardens of the Imagination cover more than six hectares of terraces on the hillside, facing the old town of Terrasson. They were opened in 1997. By designing gardens with themes referring to universal myths linked to nature, their creators fulfilled their ambition of evoking the history of humanity, without losing sight of the history of gardens. Offering visitors the pleasure of a pleasant, shady walk, decorated with fountains, games and water stairways, the Gardens of the Imagination illustrate the passionate search for a divine and enchanting paradise, between poetry and dreams, pursued through the topiary, roses and irises.

The Fountain Path

Lascaux

Since 1940 the name of Montignac has been inseparable from that of a place hitherto totally overlooked by the outside world, yet one destined to be ranked among the world's most visited tourist sites. The link was forged by a haphazard discovery made by four teenagers retrieving their overly adventurous young dog from a pothole. The discovery of the Lascaux cave is like something out of a novel, at once a miracle and one of those most fantastic tales that can be retold over and over. It should be added that what was actually discovered is every bit a match for the extraordinary stroke of luck that led to the discovery itself! The painted cave swiftly became a star attraction, so much so that abbot Breuil, an eminent specialist in prehistoric studies, visited the site and uttered the phrase that would subsequently be adopted as a publicity slogan: "Lascaux, the Sistine Chapel of Prehistory."

Everyone wanted to see Lascaux, the finest, most perfect, most extraordinary cave of them all. Between 1948 and 1963, more than one million visitors passed through Lascaux. Needless to say, a work created 17.000 years ago was deemed fragile, and precautions were duly taken. The lighting was greatly dimmed, a complex ventilation system was installed, and a dual entrance with an airlock prevented overly harsh contact with the outside atmosphere. But one million chests bring with them carbon dioxide, and moist, warm air, and air-conditioning means microbes, spores and pollen. The side-effects were more or less immediate, but it took a long while to detect them. That was when mosses and algae, admittedly microscopic, but particularly flourishing, started to cover some of the panels with a greenish film. Tremendous alarm wracked the scientific circles responsible for preserving this priceless treasure, quickly turning to panic when a follow-up diagnosis reported the outbreak of another disease,

Lascaux: Chinese horse and red cow

"white" this time, caused by the swift and irreparable deposit of white calcite on the paintings. The radical cure recommended befitted the ailment. Lascaux would have to be closed! Consternation and dismay: henceforth there would be those who have seen Lascaux, and the rest! But in due course, man's imagination joined forces with his infinite capacity for invention – sired by necessity – and twenty years later, in 1983, Lascaux II was opened. The Lascaux Cave consists of a roughly oval gallery, the Bulls' Hall, which extends into an axial room called the *Diverticule*, a narrow passage on a slight slope. To the right, it runs along a passage leading to a room called the Apse, then to a lofty gallery, the Nave, and the smaller Well Gallery, and finally to the so-called Feline Gallery. One of the quintessential physical features of Lascaux is its relatively small size. Its renown and the abundance of its drawings and paintings give it the feel of a wide, spacious cavern. In reality, and somewhat surprisingly, it is anything but this.

The Lascaux artists lived in the Upper Paleolithic period, that is during the "ancient" or "chipped" Stone Age, at the very birth of the artistic explosion of the Magdalenian. Their original art contrasts with the much more classical art found in sanctuary caves, almost invariably more recent than Lascaux.

The Bulls' Hall and the axial gallery, which can be visited in Lascaux II, are decorated with stunning paintings, blending in a riot of forms and movements the distinctive silhouettes of the Lascaux animals: a small, usually elongated head, a bulky body, short, nimble legs, horns and hooves well drawn almost face on, and thus from a different perspective than that of the body, presented in profile. Black, red and brown dominate in these magnificent compositions, where colossal bulls, their horns in three-quarter profile, launch into an endless gallop, accompanied by a series of small prancing horses, or by a host of diminutive startled stags with heavy antlers. Just one

Lascaux II

The idea of an exact replica cave, hewn out and aptly furbished in the cliff close by the "real" cave, had been simmering for some time among the team charged first with providing access to the site, and then safeguarding its treasures. It took ten years of research and hard work before Lascaux II could finally be opened to the impatient and inquisitive public. The comprehensive description of it, complete with diagrams, maps and models of how the unprecedented replica was technically constructed – the system involved recreating a three – dimensional place in its entirety – is one of the main attractions of Le Thot Centre of Prehistoric Research and Art, near Lascaux. Using the specialized method called stereophotogrammetry, the National Geographic Institute assembled thousands of photos with which to calculate the coordinates of each individual point of the cave walls. Using these data, technicians were able to make a life-size model and exact replica of the original. The only areas thus reconstructed are the rotunda called the Bulls' Hall, and Diverticule, but they are the richest. The pigments used are identical to those of Lascaux's original artists. The site accommodates some 2.000 visitors a day, and periodic restoration of the paintings is necessary to prevent the youthful "look-alike" from suffering the same fate as the original.

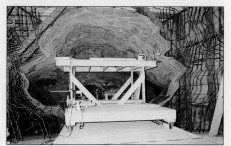

The construction of Lascaux II

creature manages to haunt the walls of this rotunda, like some mystery awaiting elucidation. This is the "unicorn", a strange, heavy-bellied beast, its round rump dappled with markings, with two gigantic, parallel ramrod horns thrusting out from its forehead. Lots of geometric symbols, points and dots, hatched and rod motifs accompany these figures, but offer no explanation as to their meaning. The paintings, mostly safely out of reach, were executed using pole scaffolding, remnants of which have also been unearthed. Oak was the most commonly used timber. A rude length of rope has also been found, confirming the very canny organization of these artists, who also fashioned their own lighting, using the famous tallow and juniper lamps, and made both their dyes and, very probably, even their own ancient brushes.

Last but not least, at the end of the long, narrow Well Gallery, not reproduced in Lascaux II but partly reproduced at Le Thot, an extraordinary scene has been drawn on the wall. A bison with a bristling mane, its side pierced by a spear, disgorges a heavy mass of entrails, and charges at a strange, schematic figure, long and lean, which has fallen over at the animal's feet. Just beside it lies a small spear thrower decorated with a beautiful bird. A nonchalant rhinoceros moves slowly away from the scene.

The arrangement of the various features as a narrative scene is exceptional in the whole of prehistoric art. If the Magdalenians had ever offered us the key to their riddle, we would perhaps be amazed by the degree of abstraction they had achieved. Like the other sanctuary caves, Lascaux clearly had a religious significance for them.

Apart from the Well scene, which is more or less intelligible, the 1500 drawings at Lascaux – animals, human beings, and geometric signs – are, for us, like so many words in an unknown language. But the syntax, in other words the commentary of the Magdalenians, will elude us forever.

Lascaux: bull

Voyage into Prehistory

This Prehistoric Research and Art Centre was opened in 1972, four miles south of Montignac, on the small hill called Le Thot, not far from the river Vézère. The educational focus of the minds behind this centre is plain to see, and a visit here makes a vital complement to your Lascaux tour. A modern, unadorned building houses the Centre of Prehistoric Research and Art, which provides visitors with every conceivable modern device for imparting knowledge. Here, you can settle yourself in a large audio-visual room where fascinating images are projected, recreating the natural prehistoric environment in which the Paleolithic fauna evolved. A survey of the famous caves at Niaux

Replica of the mammoth bone hut from Mezerich (Ukraine)

(Ariège), Altamira (Spain) and Pech-Merle (Lot) as well as Lascaux, reminds us that cave painting is not peculiar to any one region. Facsimiles and castings take us on a hazardless journey into the depths of caves that are out-of-bounds or inaccessible. Several skillfully executed Lascaux panels give a good idea of the galleries that have not been reconstructed in Lascaux II: the Well, with its scene of the bison and the wounded man, and the Nave, with its three main compositions – the Black Cow panel, the two bison, rump to rump, and the frieze of five stags emerging from a surge of dark rock. Lastly, models and photos describe in almost anatomical detail the stupendous venture represented by the birth of Lascaux II. But Le Thot is also a zoo-park, housing the direct descendants of those prehistoric creatures – aurochs, deer, horses, bison, and – surprise, surprise – lurking behind a shrub, a docile mammoth plunging his huge trunk into a small pond beside a woolly rhinoceros.

Replica of a mammoth

Losse and Belcayre

From Thonac, a road passes near La Vermondie tower before reaching Plazac. On the right bank of the Vézère, two castles guard the village: upriver, Losse castle was built in 1575 by Jean de Beaulieu de Losse. Over the river, a flattened stone archway provides a light, airy foundation. With its small round tower, its balustrades and fine mullioned windows, the castle houses a rich collection of 16th century furniture along with 17th century Dutch and Italian tapestries. Down river, Belcayre castle was built in the 15th century, and since repaired and rebuilt, occupies a rocky cliff towering above the riverbed. The main building, in a very sober architectural style, is bordered by an impressive round tower topped by a tapering, pointed roof. Near the castle, a block of rock bearing a small carved ibex has been unearthed in a rock shelter in the middle of an early Cro-Magnon settlement.

A tower with a tender heart

La Vermondie tower, surveying the river Vézère, lurks behind the thick foliage of trees lining the road. This lesser sister to that greater Tower of Pisa, with its delicate colonnades, really only bears it a likeness by the fact of the slow but relentless shift of its centre of gravity. It is a solid watch-tower, remnant of a former fortification. The blatant angle of the structure could not fail but stir people's imagination. A cruel fate dogged the pretty princess, held captive within the tower's gaol. She was lovesick for the handsome squire who would come and sing her praises at the foot of the keep. So what could be more simple for a tender-hearted tower than to lean, ever so gently, in a crazy defiance of ruin and chaos, that the lips of the two lovers might be joined in a chaste embrace... There are those who claim that, ever since those days, the tower has never managed to right itself!

Belcayre Castle

La Vermondie Tower

Saint-Léon-sur-Vézère and Sergeac

Like its big sister the Dordogne, the Vézère River follows a meandering course. In the hollow of a sweeping, wooded loop lies Saint-Léon-sur-Vézère, a village with roofs covered with dark, gnarled lauze slabs. The existence of a Benedictine priory depending on Sarlat Abbey was attested in 1153 by a bull of Pope Eugene III. It was built on the site of a Gallo-Roman villa, elements of which are visible in some sections of the former priory's base. A square bell-tower pierced by two rows of delicate arcades, and topped by a low roof with four identical faces rises above the perfect crossing of the nave and transept in this church. The chevet consists of the pure volume of its central apse and its two absidal chapels. In the centre of the village, La Salle Castle with its square 14th century keep stands next to a 15th century manor house. Near the shore of the Vézère stands 16th century Clérans Castle. A bridge spans the river and there Conquil cliff presents a fine set of overhanging rock shelters and troglodytic homes, with fortified and guard rooms, as well as storerooms. The region's inhabitants sought shelter there when danger was imminent. A pigeon-house contains no less than 148 openings. Activities like spear throwing or flint cutting are organized regularly.

On the left bank of the Vézère, Sergeac is introduced by its 16th century historiated cross. On it, Saint Michael and the Virgin surround the crucified Jesus. The lauze-roofed houses encircle a 12th century Romanesque church. A massive nave, clearly for defensive purposes, is topped with a surprising bell-tower, pierced with four arcades containing bells, as in any wall-belfry, but here they were reinforced by an actual keep lined with machicolations. All that remains is the upper fringe of the corbels.

Castel-Merle and Reverdit

Not far from Sergeac, Castel-Merle is a prehistoric site well-known for its many shelters which have yielded many valuable finds and relics. The Valley of the Rocks is lined with shelters which have yielded the oldest drawings in the world (Blanchard, Castanet and Labattut shelters). The Reverdit shelter acts as guardian to a Magdalenian frieze carved in bas-relief. During visits and tours, there are periodic flint-cutting demonstrations, showing the techniques used by prehistoric people.

The troglodytic, so-called English, fort is an interesting rock shelter, in the form of a very large natural chamber hewn out of the rock and adapted as a *cluzeau* or cliff shelter during the Middle Ages by fearful people keen to find as safe a refuge as possible.

The Sergeac Cross

La Roque-Saint-Christophe

The long limestone cliff overlooks the left bank of the river Vézère just before it meets its trubutary, the Moustier. The rock, with its varying degrees of hardness, has been scoured in long and often quite deep grooves in parallel formations, largely the work of the icy spells and thaws typical of the harsh winters of the last ice age. At the top, the lacework effect of the pale leaves of the shrubs stands out against the deep blue of the sky. Glistening green cascades of ivy cling to the face, shrouding whole stretches of white rock in the myriad highlights from the foliage. For long periods, Cro-Magnon people, 25.000 years ago, and Neolithic groups set up home beneath the rocky overhangs situated at the bottom of the cliff, at river level. In the 9th century, the natural terraces such as the great terrace of La Roque-Saint-Christophe served as one of the fortresses set up by Frotaire, Bishop of Périgueux, to combat raiding Vikings.

During the Middle Ages, people arranged these troglodytic shelters. But all that remains of these dwelling-places are the poignant signs of life hewn in the rock-face, cupboard-like structures where you can still imagine the holes for the hinges supporting the doors that closed them off; small niches where people collected the thousand and one things of everyday life; and strange rock rings, serving, no doubt, to hang lamps with their flickering flames, or attach livestock, that had to be protected at all costs. Crosses carved in the rock in what was probably a former chapel tremind us that men, women and children all lived here through difficult times and, who knows, moments of great happiness, too.

Another group of troglodytic houses, used by peasants until the early 20th century, can be seen at Cazelle, four kilometres from Les Eyzies.

The Caves of Roc de Cazelle

On the way out of Les Eyzies, on the road to Sarlat, the steep cliff of Roc de Cazelle, filled with caves, was used as a shelter, as a military camp, and as dwellings for man throughout the ages. During the Upper Paleolithic, our nomadic ancestors came there to protect themselves from the cold at the end of the Ice Age (10.000 B.C.). In the Middle Ages, the site's strategic location overlooking the Beune River valley led to its military development. Perigord peasants settled there at the beginning of the 20th century. Under the rocky shelters occupied by *Homo sapiens sapiens,* scenes from daily life in the prehistoric period have been recreated: hunting, gathering, stonecutting, wall painting, etc. Nothing is missing from the veritable troglodytic fortress dug out starting in the 10th century. Slanting corners, moats, ditches, a tunnel – all were also used during the Wars of Religion, and even by the Resistance in the Second World War. Finally, at the base of the cliff, the monolithic farm, inhabited until 1966, is moving testimony to rural life in our grandparents' time.

Scene showing a painter

La Madeleine

La Madeleine site, down river from the village of Tursac, is of paramount importance for prehistoric research.

Along this very fast-flowing loop in the river Vézère on the left bank a cliff juts out over an Upper Paleolithic site.

The wealth and sheer number of objects discovered here, back in 1863, during the initial excavations of prehistoric Perigord by E. Lartet and H. Christy, have helped to establish a scientific classification of a great age in our human saga: the "Magdalenian", so-called after the name of this site. It was a period of special importance, typified by the presence of sanctuary caves, during which the working of bone and reindeer horn achieved great perfection. Among the objects discovered miniature bison made from reindeer horn, its head tipped backward, is a masterpiece of skilled workmanship.

Above the prehistoric site, a troglodytic village clings to the rock face. People have made dwellings here since the Middle Ages, using rock shelters naturally hewn from the cliff. The entrance is designed to withstand attacks directed against this intrinsically well defended spot. A small, clear spring provides the answer to the nightmare scenario of a long siege, supplying some twenty houses with fresh water.

Like any medieval community, the village is rightly proud of its beautiful chapel with Gothic vaulting, dedicated to Saint Madeleine. To keep an eye on the river, source of all danger, a small underground passage – locally called a *cluzeau* – hewn in the soft rock, rises in the form of a watch turret towards the top of the crag. All the rich details of daily life are still visible in the dark pleats of the rock: old ovens, foundations of old doors cut in the rock, low stone walls, pipes and ducts, and fireplaces.

The whole site is dominated by the ruins of a 14th-16th century castle.

Prehistory Park at Tursac

A stone's throw from Tursac, the Prehistory Park occupies a large wooded area with footpaths and clearings. As you stroll through the cool, quiet undergrowth, you are transported pleasantly back to remote bygone times. Each display reconstructs a scene from the precarious life of Neanderthal and Cro-Magnon man. The way the places, animals and people look is not the result of the florid imagination of some over-inspired artist, but the result of the very latest anthropological research. Every detail has been deliberated over at great length, and thus remains well within the realm of the eminently probable. We proceed imperceptibly from the Mousterian period, when man did battle with huge stags, now extinct, busied himself dismembering reindeer, and negotiated the noiseless but fearsome charge of the woolly rhinoceros, to the Upper Paleolithic, when dwellings were improved as a result of a better mastery of survival techniques, as well as major advances in man's understanding of the world about him.

The mammoth hunt

Les Eyzies-de-Tayac

The little town of Les Eyzies-de-Tayac, at the confluence of the Vézère and Beune Rivers, could have kept its anonymous tranquility, like so many other pretty French villages, and also its name, Tayac, which is what it was called until the end of the 19th century. The site's beauty, the pleasant climate and wonderful food would have been largely sufficient to attract the many visitors who could have discovered the troglodytic shelters or the castle, owned by the Beynac family, arranged in the cliffs during the troubled days of the Middle Ages. They could also admire the fortified church of Saint Martin of Tayac, dating from the 12th century, in whose walls and portal the builders reused stones from pre-Roman, Carolingian and Gallo-Roman times. However, the first settlers in Perigord, over 350.000 years ago, had decided otherwise. And the *Primitive Man*, a statue by Paul Dardé inaugurated in 1931, standing in front of the National Museum of Prehistory and overlooking the village and the valley, is there to remind us, if necessary, that these inhabitants of Perigord in the Middle and Upper Paleolithic periods chose to settle there. Just before the Vézère River joins the Dordogne, it has carved out its own valley in a limestone massif filled with caves, lined with high cliffs with overhanging shelters and rock ledges. Man had to protect himself from the harsh cold that froze the steppe landscape with its low trees stretching as far as the eye could see. The shallow hollows in the cliff, warmed by the wan rays of the sun and protected by branches covered with hides and furs, provided temporarily-occupied shelters, when he did not set up camp in open areas. Excavations began in 1863. Thousands of tons of earth were sifted, thousands of objects were classified, labelled, hundreds of sketches were deciphered and analyzed. Some of the

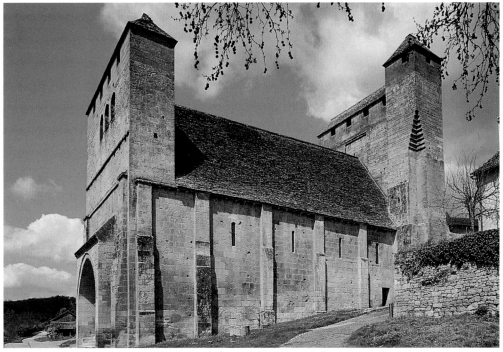

Les Eyzies-de-Tayac: fortified church in Tayac

objects brought to light during excavations are on display at the museum at the Pataud Shelter and at the National Museum of Prehistory. The excavations have led to the discovery of over a hundred sites in the lower Vézère valley.

In the village of Les Eyzies, in 1868 the Cro-Magnon Shelter revealed the existence of a new stage in human evolution. Five skeletons ornamented with jewels and shells, including a particularly well-preserved one of an *old man* about forty to fifty years old, characterize Cro-Magnon Man. A *Homo sapiens sapiens*, thirty-five thousand years old, he was the first modern man, similar to us both physically and intellectually.

South of the village, La Mouthe was the first decorated cave discovered in Dordogne in 1895. In addition to numerous engraved animals, one of the walls contains a mystery, a kind of "hut", one of those geometric signs which, like all the abstract markings represented in these caves, is difficult to interpret.

Halfway between Les Eyzies and Le Bugue, on the right bank of the Vézère, Saint Cirq cave contains Magdalenian representations: ibex, horses and bison and, of course, the strange "Sorcerer". The word sorcerer is a misleading term for this human silhouette which retains all its mystery. Still on the right bank, but upriver, several sites surround the Grand Roc cave. The Fish Shelter owes its name to a Gravetian engraving of a salmon. The Laugerie-Haute deposit, occupied 20.000 years ago and abandoned during the Magdalenian period, presents a fine section of stratigraphy. The deposit at Laugerie-Basse contained Magdalenian, Neolithic and Gallo-Roman vestiges. The Rock of Tayac is both a troglodytic fort and a pleasant speleological museum. As for the La Micoque deposit, its occupation dates back over 300.000 years. In this cradle of human settlement in Perigord, there are no traces of fire having been used during the early occupation of the site.

The Fish Shelter: the salmon

The prehistoric deposit in the Pataud Shelter

To discover properly what a prehistoric dwelling-place was like, and how these dwellings are studied on an archaeological site, you would do well to venture into the Pataud shelter. This rock shelter was inhabited for 15.000 years at the start of the Upper Paleolithic. The excavations have yielded a series of 14 levels of dwellings, clearly identifiable in the banks of earth not yet cleared – on the spot evidence of an extremely rich stratigraphy. There is a display of the excavator's equipment – a fine-bristled broom, a small knife, a small brush to clear the surface and remove, grain by grain, the matrix of hardened earth that has protected these treasures for thousands of years. The Pataud Shelter Museum, attached to the National Museum of Natural History, and a research centre in its own right, offers even uninitiated visitors a rich source of information, aided by very modern technology. Stratigraphy – a thankless and often even dull science – becomes as clear as daylight here, thanks to small video systems where cartoons combined with simple but detailed explanations finally reveal the secrets of an exciting branch of knowledge. Human remains, tools, and unearthed objects are all on display, and the very ceiling of the museum – once a prehistoric shelter itself, and only much later turned into a troglodytic cave – features one of the earliest known bas-relief sculptures, a charming little ibex, cleverly shown to best advantage by an ingenious system of mirrors and lighting. Last of all, there is the pensive, almost beautiful statue of a young Perigord girl, some 20.000 years old, who died when barely sixteen. This statue has been modelled from anthropological data gathered from a skeleton discovered on this very site.

Reconstitution of a 16 year-old Cro-Magnon

An ibex (as seen in a mirror)

The National Museum of Prehistory

It was within the framework of protecting the local heritage that, in 1913, the creation of a National Museum of Prehistory was planned in Les Eyzies de Tayac. At the beginning of the 20th century, the Vézère River valley – an Eldorado for scholars of prehistory – was being looted by the less scrupulous ones. Several of the most prestigious objects disappeared abroad or at private collectors'. A schoolteacher in Les Eyzies, Denis Peyrony (1869-1954), already an acknowledged expert in prehistory, entered the fray. He simultaneously defended instituting laws to protect archaeological sites and founding an establishment where excavated objects could be deposited. Arranged within the vestiges of a 16th century castle, which had itself been built on a site occupied by Magdalenians 12.000 years ago, the storehouse was enlarged with a museum whose first rooms opened in 1918, before the official inauguration in 1923. As new discoveries were made, the collections increased in size, requiring the development of new showrooms. This is the background to the new National Museum of Prehistory of Les Eyzies, built according to a design by the architect J-P Buffi, which opened in July, 2004, under the watchful eye of Primitive Man, whose massive, durable statue has been watching over the location since 1931. At the same time a place of memory for the history of prehistory and a place to preserve objects, the museum of Les Eyzies, with its 5 million objects of which 18.000 are on display, today contains one of the most important Paleolithic collections in the world. The entrance hall

is dedicated to the theme of the rise of Man, described in an "anthropological frieze". Then, a corridor carved out of the rock face of the cliff shows the visitor the history of the first hominids, this "African history". This history leads from the *Australopithecus* Lucy who lived 3.500.000 million years ago – a life-like "recreation" based on her skeleton found in Ethiopia in 1974 is presented – to the reconstitution of the adolescent of Lake Turkana, a *Homo ergaster* or *Homo erectus* who lived in Kenya 1.800.000 million years ago. The collections of the flint and bone tools in the lower gallery are organized along two axes: a longitudinal timeline from the early Paleolithic (350.000 years ago) to the end of the Ice Ages (10.000 years ago), presenting reconstitutions of *Megaceros* and a woolly rhinoceros; and the transversal axis that

Bison licking its side, La Madeleine Shelter

The sorcerer, La Madeleine Shelter

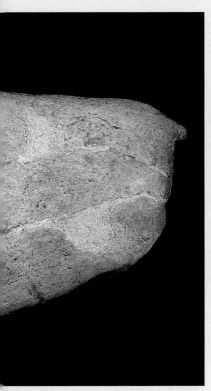

Block decorated
with a horse,
La Madeleine Shelter

follows the evolution of cultures, from the Neanderthals to the Magdalenian people. The upper gallery, dedicated to the way of life and habitat, offers the visitor a journey within a prehistoric space, from the exterior, with its reconstructed open-air sites such as stone-cutting workshops, towards the interior, with its reconstructed hearths and the presentation of art objects, ornaments or furniture, and finally, human burial places. The product of the collaboration and work of devoted specialists, the Les Eyzies Museum is also a study centre. It contains one of the most important international libraries specializing in the field of prehistory, and its laboratory team works steadfastly to recognize and evaluate archaeological remains, participates in excavations and publishes periodicals, including the review *Paléo*, and monographs.

Laurel leaf,
Le Pech de La Boissière

129

Commarque and Laussel

Commarque is undoubtedly the finest ruin in the region. Once a castle bristling with huge fortifications, it now peers up at the firmament through the strange gaping holes of its roofless buildings. The already complicated layout of its architecture is further confused by the jumble of rubble, giving a glimpse, here, of the elegant span of an arch plunging against the sky, and, there, of sheer, dizzy-making stairways, as if clinging to the sky's edge, and fireplaces staring on to the void. Commarque is the epitome of a ruined castle, at once shadowy and haughty. The stronghold was abandoned in the early 17th century, and its architecture has not been touched or altered since. The greater part of the old castle dates back to the 12th century. A fief of the Commarque family, then the Beynacs, it was a fully fortified village capable of affording shelter not only to the lord's family, but to several peasant families as well.

Here we can still see the chapel built over a postern gate, and there the bread oven in the baker's house. In the 15th century, with the end of the Hundred Years' War, a new main building was erected within the castle walls, opening on to the valley through large mullioned windows.

By comparison, and as if to underscore the irrevocable destruction of Commarque, Laussel Castle a possession of the Commarques, then the Beynacs, seems quite alive. With its handsome keep enhanced by machicolations, its round towers, its long protective walls and its inner baileys and yards, it was built in several stages from the 15th to the 17th centuries. It is at the prehistoric site of Laussel, a stone's throw from the castle, where it the famous figure of the *Horned Venus* was unearthed. In her left hand she holds a strange object shaped like a cow's horn. Overall, she presents a heavy figure, where womanliness and, more particularly, motherhood have been sublimated.

Commarque Castle

The Prehistoric Sites in the Beunes Valleys

Combarelles Cave: a lion's head

The main Beune river and its tributary, the Little Beune meet the Vézère at Les Eyzies. They, too, guard treasures buried in their steep banks – traces of post–Lascaux art on rock walls. The Font-de-Gaume Cave has a huge, sunny 'porch', giving access to a tunnel that winds over 100 metres into the cliff. Several passages run off it. On the far side of a cramped, narrow passage, 'Rubicon' like in its implication and with reddish signs, the cave broadens and is decorated with paintings many thousands of years old. On the yellow ochre walls, the Magdalenians – a Cro-Magnon group – painted and carved one of the most remarkable series of animals. The creatures square up against or pursue one another, while some are superimposed. Here we see cumbersome bison with bulging backs, a drawing of two clashing reindeer, identifiable by their long antlers, and long-tusked mammoths. In places, calcite has laid a still translucent layer over the powerful, clearly defined depiction of a horse at the gallop, now fading irrevocably. The bison is the best represented animal in this cave, where, with a skill that astounds (but only because we wrongly imagine these ancestors to have been ham-fisted people), these artists cleverly recreated the energy, life and brute force of a herd. With foreheads lowered, keen, dark eyes staring at the target of a premeditated gallop, horns gracefully curved, lips drooping and panting, the multi-coloured bison of Font-de-Gaume are veritable masterpieces. Not far from here, the Les Combarelles Cave is an art gallery, no more no less, extending along a 300 metre passage. In cave art sites, the carvings and drawings often increase in number and decorativeness, the further one ventures from the entrance. This is very much the case here, and over the last 100 metres we find a hotch-potch explosion of drawings, inextricably entangled, and forming one large single masterpiece. Every animal is there: mammoths, bison, reindeer, horses, ibex... But just as Rouffignac is the mammoths' cave, so Les Combarelles would seem to be the horses'. There are more than 100 depictions, but few explanations for this phenomenon. One or two life-like animal postures indicate the keen sense of observation of which our forbears were capable. A reindeer, for example, neck

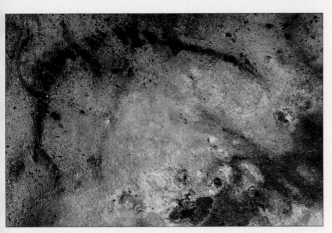

another prehistoric site open to the public. Here, Magdalenian camps have been found (flint and bone), but, more importantly, the rock shelter that protected them, renowned for its fine frieze carved beneath the jutting 'eaves' of a broad limestone awning. More than 14 metres of rock have been worked in high relief, that is, deeply carved and sculpted, to render as salient as possible the elegant forms of four life-size horses and a few bison and reindeer. The realism and vitality of the figures stem undoubtedly from the fact that the

outstretched, with large antlers, poised on its legs, is undoubtedly in the process of drinking. There are plenty of human, or at least anthropomorphic, figures and geometric signs. But just as the relevant choice of an essential detail helps to clearly identify a particular animal, so the extremely schematic figures leave us without any explanation as to the purpose of these representations. Further upstream, the Cap-Blanc shelter is

Font-de-Gaume Cave: a bison's head

Le Cap-Blanc Shelter: a horse

Magdalenian artist painstakingly polished the sculpted volumes and successfully integrated them in the contours of the wall, to underscore the line of the hindquarters, musculature and heads. The small Bernifal Cave, in the Little Beune valley, also boasts, among a host of dots, lines and geometric signs (the "roof-shaped" series are noteworthy), several mammoth figures, and fine drawings of bison and horses.

Grand Roc Cave

At the foot of the white façade of a cliff capped by dense, gently rolling woodland, Grand Roc cave looks out over the calm and peaceful landscape of the Vézère valley. A man-made tunnel, some 40 metres long, offers access to a veritable geode hewn out by seeping water that has gradually dissolved the limestone. The whole effect is one of unusual beauty. There are stalactites and stalagmites in abundance, and down the millennia, nature has been busily at work as a goldsmith. The hugely varied shapes and sizes of the formations, thrusting into space their slender, translucent needles, create a fairyland setting. There are countless, aptly named, eccentric formations, too. These are small, crazily-shaped concretions, obeying laws that at first glance seem contradictory, gathered in beautiful clusters of decorative pins, where, at random, the fine crystalline projections have been scattered in a thousand different directions. This strange natural creation has been compared with the exuberant forms of coral, where every upright stem becomes the base of a new mineral spray, culminating in an apparently chaotic and inextricable tangle. Yet the laws of physics which govern such crystallizations obey an inner mathematical rigour which leaves no room for creativity or fantasy. As in the chasm of Proumeyssac, the rock crystallizations take on this amazing shape of small triangles, arranged pell-mell, at the bottom of tiny transparent pools.

The natural cave known as Carpe Diem is a narrow, twisting tunnel, some 200 metres in length. The cave conceals lots of concretions, and, in particular, a series of stalagmites and stalactites adorned with the loveliest of colours offered by the chemical action of water slowly seeping through a rock ceiling. The dissolving process carried out by the water releases mineral substances with iridescent hues.

Grand Roc Cave: the coral-like eccentrics

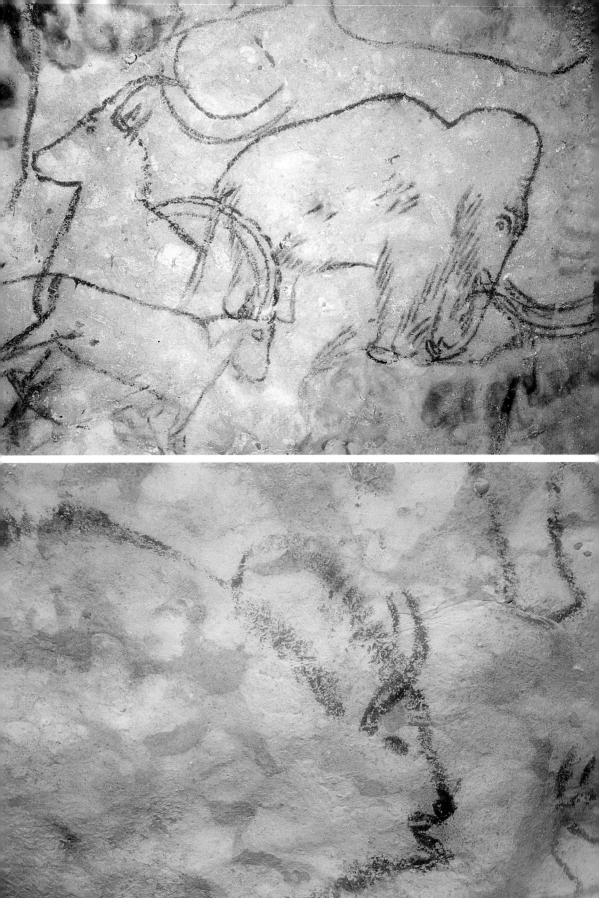

Rouffignac

In the martyred village of Rouffignac, destroyed in 1944, only the small church remains. Its belfry-porch has a doorway decorated in the 16th century with Corinthian-style, not to say oriental capitals. It is adorned with beautiful Gothic vaulting, in the pure Flamboyant style, supported by slender carved columns. The choir is Romanesque. But the village is most well-known for its extraordinary "cave of the 100 mammoths". This is a vast network of tunnels, more than 10 kilometres long, hewn in the soft rock by a large underground river. In the roof of the vaults, many impressive "giants' kettles" have been carved out by the strength of the swirling currents imprisoned in the rock. On the ground, now completely dry, large bears hibernated during the Würm glaciation. They have left behind countless traces made by their claws on the walls. The cave has had visitors since the 16th century, as is attested to by the graffiti which spoil the walls. In 1957, the engravings and paintings were identified and authenticated by R. Nougier and abbot Breuil. Almost 200 drawings and engravings produced some 12.000 years ago cover these walls. All the animals traditionally depicted by the Magdalenians are here: bison, horses, and huge woolly rhinoceroses, several "roof-shaped" or tectiform signs. But the majority of representations are of mammoths. With confident strokes, those ancient people sketched the silhouettes, postures and gestures of those wonderful creatures, which were already on the road to extinction. The huge and imposing "Patriarch", and the two great herds fiercely vying with each other seem to defy time. There are many friezes showing mammoths, ibex, bison, and horses, but the most outstanding is the one on the ceiling of the last "Great Hall". This is a unique composition, where the silhouettes interlock and demand an extreme concentration to unravel the tangle of superposed lines.

Rouffignac Cave: a carved horse

In the land of Jacquou le Croquant

Between Rouffignac and la Manoire, a tributary of the Auvézère river, the Barade forest, L'Herme Castle and the village of Fanlac inspired the decor of Eugène Le Roy's novel *Jacquou le Croquant*. Eugène Le Roy was born on 29 November 1836 in Hautefort. His father was the castle steward, and Eugène himself became the tax collector in Hautefort in 1893. His most famous novel is beyond any dispute *Jacquou Le Croquant,* published in 1899. The adaptation of the book, into a television series in 1969, allowed the general public to discover this masterpiece of 19th century literature. Jacquou is a man whose aspirations, energies, and sensibilities correspond so closely to those of the small share-croppers or day-labourers in the wretched conditions of the Perigord countryside in the 19th century, that he has become their image and symbol. His father, Martin Ferral, is a share-cropper of the lord of Nansac. For all their exhausting labours, Jacquou's family plunges into ever deeper poverty. Beside himself, and unable to put up with these injustices a day longer, his father kills the lord's estate manager in a righteous fit of anger. This marks the start of a long odyssey for young Jacquou, who sees his father hauled off to penal servitude and his mother die from exhaustion. Taken in by the vicar of Fanlac, he becomes a handsome and well-educated young man, but one who

L'Herm Castle: the Gothic Doorway

L'Herm Castle

L'Herm Castle:
detail of vault
in spiral staircase

problem besetting the 19th century peasantry was not the nobility but…taxes! These days, L'Herm Castle is no more than a castle fallen from grace. Hidden in thick woodland, the white-stone structure consists of a three-storey main building, with two round towers to the west, and a distinctive hexagonal staircase tower to the east. The entrance is a gem, a subtle mixture of flamboyant Gothic lavishness and Renaissance refinement. The sculpted recessed vaults cross in diagonal arches, and the upper archway, laden with the intricate finery of kale motifs, ends in a four-centered arch extended by a long pinnacle-shaped arrow. Many overly fragile details have vanished or been damaged, but the overall effect is one of rare beauty. The main doorway gives on to a spiral stairway whose central pillar is a masterpiece of craftsmanship. The pillar is embellished by rope moulding, and seems to coil about itself with infinite elegance, right to the topmost burst of its graceful fan vault. The main building has lost its roof and all its ceilings, but it has kept the sculptures of its huge fireplaces still embedded in the walls bearing the Calvimont's coat of arms. In 1512, Jean III de Calvimont was president of the Bordeaux parliament, before being named ambassador to Charles V in 1526. He was assassinated, as was his daughter, in 1605, by her own husband, François d'Aubusson. Its troubled and eventful history has lent it a sinister reputation, which the charming poetry of its walls has not altogether managed to dispel. Fanlac has a Romanesque Church with the wall-belfry. The "Jacquou House" in Combenègre was used in the film of the novel. And the 12th century Romanesque church in Plazac stands next to the former residence of the bishops of Sarlat.

has retained a very keen awareness of the injustice inherent in a society founded upon the inequality of man. In his own turn, he pits himself against the Nansac family, and with the help of the peasants living in Barade forest, manages to destroy that symbol of arrogance and dread, L'Herm Castle. The impressive ruins of L'Herm have nothing to do with these imagined ravages, but they offered Eugène Le Roy an obvious source of inspiration. E. le Roy Ladurie – author of the classic, *Montaillou* – has analysed this book, reminding us that the real

Le Bugue

The town of Le Bugue, nestling in the crook of a loop of the Vézère River, a few kilometres from the Vézère-Dordogne confluence, was already during the Roman period a stopping-point on the road linking Périgueux to Cahors. In 964, the Benedictine abbey founded by Grimoald and Adelaide of Montignac turned the town into an important urban centre. In homage to the lords of Limeuil, in exchange for their protection, Le Bugue owed them submission. Few vestiges remain from that period, other than the Bas Mill. During the 13th century, it was called Got Mill and belonged to Bugue Abbey; from the 16th century until the Revolution, it was the property of the lords of Limeuil. Each year, Le Bugue celebrates the alleged visit of King Louis IX to the small town. The king, who was to become Saint Louis, is also linked to development of the local heritage. The fish in the Aquarium of Black Perigord come from rivers in Perigord, but also elsewhere in France and Europe. The village of Bournat brings back to life rural activities and occupations. As for the Arborie Gardens, besides an arboretum, they present miniature Perigord-style architecture.

Upriver from the town, on the left bank of the Vézère, the present Campagne Castle, state property, dates partly from the 15th century, but mostly from the 18th.

On the way out of Le Bugue, on the road to Lalinde, the engravings of Bara-Bahau Cave were discovered by N. Casteret and his daughter in 1951. The cave is a wide, 100 metre-long gallery dug out by an underground river from very crumbly rock, made up of clay and chalk, containing thousands of flint nodules. Cave bears hibernated here and have left traces made by their claws. The Magdalenians who followed them were quick to take advantage of such a soft surface. Using flint tools, or simply with sticks,

The Arborie Gardens

A thousand trees and bushes and two thousand succulent plants, combining the rarest and the most original, make up the great variety of plants in the Arborie Gardens, created in 1994. But these gardens are more than just an ordinary botanical park. The strange and the unusual abound in this landscape where giant vegetables mingle with dwarf trees. In your rendez-vous with the marvellous, you end up losing all sense of proportion; you might even end up feeling as if you'd drunk some magic potion and turned into a giant come to take a casual stroll through Perigord. For the landscape's composition plays with scale by recreating the realistic environment of the Perigourdian countryside in Lilliputian dimensions. Castles and traditional stone houses with their high, tiled roofs are reduced to a scale of 1/20th. They even have their own parks where the bonsai trees with which they are landscaped cast just the right amount of shade on their miniature lawns.

The Arborie Gardens

they engraved thousands of enigmatic signs in grids, but also a phallus and several animal representations: horses, aurochs, bison, reindeer and even the forequarters of a bear. Perched on a promontory at the confluence of the Vézère and Dordogne rivers, the steep narrow streets of Limeuil still retain a medieval atmosphere. The Romanesque church of Saint Martin stands in the cemetery. It was consecrated in 1194. A text carved into a stone indicates that Thomas à Becket was one of the patrons of the shrine and that Richard the Lionheart was one of its founders, although the latter's father, Henry II, had had Becket murdered in Canterbury Cathedral in 1170. The houses with their ornate pediments, the ramparts and fortified gates, underscore the village's key defensive role. Two stone bridges, each spanning one of the rivers at their meeting point, nearly form a right angle. Over a hundred limestone slabs decorated with fine Magdalenian engravings depicting horses, reindeer and bulls, have been unearthed beneath the village. They are now displayed in various museums. Above Limeuil, naturalists and gourmets will find an interesting garden-museum.

North-west of Limeuil, the church of Saint Martial of Paunat used to be the abbey church of a monastery founded in the 8th century and attached to Saint Martial's Abbey of Limoges at the beginning of the 9th century. The belfry-porch, the transept and choir date from the 12th century; the nave was transformed in stages between the 14th and 17th centuries. Strong-rooms were fitted in the extrados of the vaults of the choir, the transept and the belfry. The church's fortifications are also evident in its high walls reinforced by buttress, and its steeple that looks like a keep. Despite its defensive elements, the church suffered violence and destruction from the time of Viking raids, through the English occupation during the Hundred Years War, until Protestant looting in the 16th century.

La Ferrassie

Located three kilometres from Le Bugue on the road to Rouffignac, La Ferrassie site was unearthed during road construction and excavated from 1902 to 1921 by Denis Peyrony, the schoolteacher from Eyzies. Through its protective railings, this vast rock shelter displays an interesting stratification, or superposition of its sedimentary layers revealing the different stages of the site's occupation. First Neanderthals and then the Cro-Magnons inhabited the shelter, leaving behind numerous traces of their presence. This rare consistancy of occupation has turned La Ferrassie site into a reference for the establishment of Mousterian and Aurignacian typologies. The earth also revealed valuable evidence of the spirituality of the Neanderthals, who were the first people to bury their dead. The remains of two adults, a man and a woman, three children aged from ten, three and two years old along with two newborns and a foetus had been buried for over 40.000 years in pits dug in the shelter's ground. Finally, a collection of stone blocks, engraved or painted, were also unearthed. An example of Cro-Magnon art, these vulvar and animal figures typical of Aurignacian culture are on view at the Eyzies' museum.

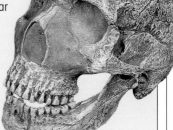

Skull of Neanderthal Man

The Black Perigord Aquarium

To offer the spectacle of the aqualic world to the public while respecting the living conditions of the fish, this is the challenge undertaken by the Black Perigord Aquarium. Decorated by abundant plantings, the sixteen large-sized tanks fed by a water-table recreate the specific environments of the different species: the warm, stagnant water of ponds for carp and tench; the cool, running water of rivers for trout and salmon. The natural living conditions are respected in these open air tanks and the fish follow their own biological cycles according to the sun and the seasons. There is the carp, for example, which hibernates in silt. They are also able to freely hunt the insects which land on the surface or find themselves the prey of birds, kingfishers, herons, and cormorants. To ensure the good health of their

The tunnel

Trout

boarders, a team of scientists and technicians regularly monitor the quality of the water, which is constantly renewed, and watch over reproduction and possible pathologies. There are even separate ponds providing a rest home for aging fish. Visitors are able to enter the very heart of the aquatic world thanks to a glass-walled tunnel three hundred metres long which withstands the pressure of more than seven hundred thousand litres of water. It is fascinating to see the often inaccessible aquatic habitat, which, seen from inside, opens up strange and marvellous views of a sadly unfamiliar world. The under-water walkway provides a near direct contact with the fish and the most common species from European rivers are discovered in a new way; perch and pike, for example, or the more spectacular two metre long silurid. As for the fish from more distant warm waters, such as koï carp or Mongolian tench, they easily stand out from their European cousins with their exquisitely bright colours.

The Village of Bournat

A life which follows the measured beat of craftsmen's gestures, the streets filled with the aroma of fresh baked bread, the villagers meeting up at the coffeehouse counter... the simple things of daily life which our great-grandfathers experienced, destined to disappear and which the farm-Village of Bournat is attempting to salvage. It is not a museum but a real Perigourdian village, the way so many used to be at the end of the 19th century. Set on the banks of the Vézère, the traditional houses built out of stone and roofed with *lauzes* echo with activity. For this is a place where memory is kept alive. Surrounded by the tools and old objects presented in their everyday context, the life of yesteryear seems to reappear. In their workshops, artisans keep a savoir-faire alive and invite visitors to discover or rediscover ancient, often forgotten trades. The blacksmith, the cobbler, the saddler, the wood carver, or the cooper... fifteen or so trades in all, which used to be indispensable to life in a village, are depicted.

The washing-place

There are many animals raised on the farm which lives according to the rhythm of harvests from the fields and vegetable garden. Bees attend to their laborious activity in transparent hives. The woodsaw is powered by a steam engine, the bread is baked in a wood oven and the oil produced in a walnut mill according to the local tradition. Even a barber is prepared to give you a close shave in a corner of the bar. Nostalgia must strike some in front of the school entrance where a dictation excercise awaits you and certainly the sight of the fortune teller's caravan will awaken a hope or two. There is no doubt that young and old will find themselves at the funfair, some enchanted by the discovery of an unknown world, others immersed in a sweet memory or two...

A steam locomotive

Proumeyssac Chasm

In the thick limestone formations along the Vézère valley, not far from where it meets the river Dordogne, there is a large cavern gouged from the rock mass, ever so slowly down the ages, by infiltrating water. It is called Proumeyssac chasm. The outcome of this process shows what the combination of water's mechanical and chemical forces can do. A "giant's kettle" has been hollowed out in the form of an enormous air bubble, linked with the plateau's surface by a narrow hole.

It was through this hole, conveyor since the Middle Ages of all the ills visited from the other world, peopled with the devil's vile creatures, that a well-digger dared to venture in 1907. Down into the *Cro de Promeissat* he went, in a simple bucket attached to a winch. It took his breath away immediately. The size of the "hole", and the crystalline beauty of its walls, would very soon transform it from the fuming mouth of hell into a wonderful underground attraction, in due course available for viewing on guided visits. In those days, the same system of access was used – a wooden gondola, all very Jules Verne, firmly attached to ropes gliding smoothly on a winch. Clutching the edge of the light basket, two or three people could make a particularly thrilling descent into the dark bowels of the earth. This rudimentary but efficient system was used from 1924 to 1952.

In 1957 it was decided to dig a convenient access tunnel, designed for even the most timorous of visitors, half way up – or down – the chasm. To the strains of gentle music, the play of light and shadow begins, stirring up the suspense of the imminent discovery by a canny admixture of sparkling jets of clarity and diffused stroking motions of subtle chiaroscuro effects. Under this clever lighting, the walls of the chasm undulate, swell, shrink and no longer obey any elementary law of natural physics whatsoever. The effect is gripping.

Next, the chasm offers us the dulcet murmuring of its waters, because it breathes, whispers and drips in a thousand babbling rivulets. The water, filtered by the huge rock masses that it has to seep through, reappears here, limpid and clear at the bottom of natural basins with bluish highlights, delimited by rims of pale rock.

And yet this water cannot be called pure water. It is saturated with calcium carbonate, and so lines the chasm with its aerial compositions. Four evenly trickling fountains emerge halfway up the chasm. Wherever it emerges, on the impressive mantle of smooth rock, the water deposits invisible particles of calcite which creep as far as the intricate fringe of the stone hangings suspended gracefully in the void.

No two fountains are alike. There is the Medusa, broad and heavy, dripping with the regular plash of a small waterfall; and the slender Mermaid, extending in a series of swellings to its final point. All are lively and active, and are plain evidence that this is definitely "poetry in motion". Water does not miss a stitch in the skillful tapestries of its concretions, which capture its full power. At the bottom of the chasm, ledges have been made, bearing hundreds of pieces of pottery, also undergoing the labours of water.

But the chasm also offers a show of stalactites, serried rows of them, long and tapering, like lances thrust towards the ground, sharp and menacing.

You have to stoop low and walk bent double beneath the upturned tips of this gigantic fakir's bed, if you want to reach the marvel of marvels, well hidden in the crystalline depths of the rock – the famous "triangles". Under a thin layer of limpid water, they are tiny. Nature has accustomed us to geometric constructions, where the curved line is nonetheless master. Here, to the contrary, she busies herself drawing straight lines, and, with a perfect grasp of the great theorems of applied physics, she builds magnificent little triangles of rock.

5

IN THE HEART OF PERIGORD

Périgueux

As capital of the Dordogne, Périgueux is every bit a match for the rich provinces around it when it comes to ancient historical remains. The south bank of a meander in the river Isle, hewn and hollowed, offers ideal high ground, duly and swiftly transformed into a hill fort by the Gallic Petrocorii. But the oldest traces of settlement here date back to prehistoric times. The Petrocorii or "four tribes" were unable to stem the tide of Roman legions, and yielded to the superior might of the invaders. This marked the start of the *Pax romana*, undeniably imposed and suffered as the outcome of the Gallic defeat, but at the same time ushering in a period of peace and prosperity which would see the construction of a magnificent Gallo-Roman town in the plain. Like all the major provinces of the Roman Empire, the province of Aquitaine was divided into units called a *civitas*. Artful in politics, the Romans overlaid their own organization on the ancient territories dominated by the various Gallic tribes. The realm of the Petrocorii became the *civitas petrocoriorum*. Invariably well disposed towards a smooth assimilation of the indigenous peoples in their power, the Romans were always extremely careful in their choice of the best sites and their denomination. The small hill fort, which was too cramped on the south bank of the Isle, was gradually abandoned, and the huge tongue of gently sloping land, swaddled by the calm-flowing river Isle, offered what seemed an ideal place for building the capital of the *civitas* of the Petrocorii. A local deity called *Vesunna*, already welcomed into the most hospitable arms of the Roman pantheon, would lend the place its name. *Vesona* grew, prospered, and grew

some more. It had everything: a beautiful forum, an amphitheatre, temples, basilicas, plush residences, and even an impressive aqueduct to feed the hot baths and fountains dear to these refugees from a pure Mediterranean civilization. This period of unruffled prosperity saw the building of the splendid amphitheatre, somewhat too quickly christened *les arènes* or bullring in French. Now, sadly, all that remains are a few thick walls, well preserved in a splendid park. The masonry remains still existing on the surface attest to and give an idea of the colossal size of the foundations and basements buried underground. Twenty thousand people could be seated on the stone tiers. The villa of Pompeius, in effect a grand *domus* or dwelling, also dates from the 1st century B.C. It surrounds the well-preserved remains of a colonnaded peristyle, and has all the features of a Roman house. Beautiful frescoes with plant and geometric motifs cover the walls of the sixty or so small living rooms. The hypocaust heating system, using a network of ducts made of refractory bricks linked to a central furnace and fuelled constantly by firewood, came in most handy in a region where the winters can sometimes be harsh. The low brick pillars supporting the paving-stones are still visible, and the sheer number of rooms that received heating suggests that one whole wing might have been used to house hot baths and a pool decorated with mosaics. Vesona's tower is the impressive remains of a round temple dedicated to the deity. You should imagine it surrounded by porticoes with slender colonnades and its elegant peristyle borrowing support from it. When it was covered with slabs of marble – now no longer there – it must have been a grandiose building. And even if it has been reduced to the simple cylindrical architecture of

Vesunna, the Gallo-Roman Museum of Périgueux

The main town of the *civitas* of the Petrocorii, one of the twenty-one towns that made up the great province of Aquitaine, created by Augustus (27 B.C. – 14 A.D.), *Vesunna* (the former name of the city of Périgueux) was founded in about 16 B.C. on the right bank of the Isle River, within the wide loop formed by it. It enjoyed three centuries of prosperity before being partly dismantled when, at the end of the 3rd century, it was enclosed by thick ramparts built using the stone blocks of the monuments that remained outside them. The best-preserved Gallo-Roman town of Aquitaine, *Vesunna* well deserved having a museum dedicated to it. This has finally been accomplished with the opening in July, 2003 of Vesunna, the Gallo-Roman Museum in Périgueux, located in the heart of the ancient town, a few steps from the Tower of Vesona – a vestige of the sacred heart, the *cella,* of the immense sanctuary that the Petrocorii raised to the Celtic goddess Vesunna, after whom the town was named. Vesunna is an on-site museum. Its fine glass and steel architecture, designed by Jean Nouvel, protects and displays the remains of a vast and wealthy Gallo-Roman dwelling to its advantage. This is the Vesona *domus,*

discovered in 1959. Remarkable because of its size, about 4.000 square metres, the site of the *domus* in fact corresponds to the space occupied by two houses built one after the other. The first, built in the 1st century A.D. around a peristyle, was filled up to a depth of about a metre during the 2nd century, for unknown reasons. On top of it, a second house was then built with a nearly identical layout but enriched with two peristyles in the north, private baths were fitted, an a system of heating through hypocausts was installed. The filling up of the first house preserved an exceptional collection of wall paintings dating from the reign of the Emperor Claudius, in about 40-50 A.D. Corresponding to the lower sections of the frescoes that decorated the rooms of the first *domus,* these paintings present

Moulded sigillate ceramic, 90-120 A.D.

Wall painting, mid-1st century

150

essentially geometric designs, characteristic of the "third Pompey style". The fish fresco, which dates from the middle of the 2nd century and shows Mediterranean marine animals on an ochre background, used to be located on the garden wall of the second house. Walking around the *domus* on wooden walkways, the visitor discovers its various areas within which the principal aspects of daily life during the Gallo-Roman period are treated thematically: washing and finery in the bathing area, the meals near the kitchen, and so on. Beforehand, the visitor can discover ancient *Vesunna* in the two rooms on the mezzanine floor arranged in the western wing of the museum. They contain a permanent exhibition about Vesona, in particular an interesting collection of carved stones from the ramparts of the end of the 3rd century.

Detail of fish fresco, mid-2nd century

Detail of taurobolic altar, 2nd-3rd centuries

A *pantheios* divinity, bronze, 1st-2nd centuries

151

a truncated tower, disembowelled by a fatal breach, it is still one of the finest reminders of the Gallo-Roman town of Vesona. But the calm and tranquil life of the small town enclosed in the soft cocoon of an Empire at the height of its power was doomed not to last. Ever dangerous Barbarian forays across the imperial frontiers would upset the town's customs and aspect. From the 3rd century on, Vesona cowered behind solid ramparts. To build these walls, strong enough to withstand all manner of onslaught, there were stones aplenty. All you had to do was dismantle them from the stately monuments that were once the glory of the place. The temples were demolished and the amphitheatre, with its thick walls, transformed into a bastion. This Gallo-Roman wall is still clearly visible today from the rue Turenne or towards the fortified so-called Norman Gate. Shafts of columns, heavy flagstones, lintels, carved capitals, all were incorporated in the most disparate stone construction, which ended up being almost 20 feet thick. But the stone walls were no longer enough to protect it from successive waves of Alemanni, Visigoths and Franks. Vesona was no longer a capital wielding authority over a frightened land. It lost its privileges, and even its sonorous Latin name, which dissolved into the vague and general tag of "town of the Petrocorii", and in due course ended up as no more than "Town". The place then went through centuries of thankless, cold recession. True, it was the seat of the bishopric founded by Saint Front, apostle of Perigord, but it was now merely the heart of the county of Perigord, as it gingerly approached the feudal era. Barrière Castle is the remains of one of those fortified dwellings that bolstered the town ramparts. The Christian fervour of the inhabitants of the region was heartened by the presence of the tomb of Saint Front. As the goal of a thriving pilgrimage, the tomb quickly became encompassed by the protective ecclesiastical buildings of a monastery, and by the slightly disorderly but more and more well-to-

On the road to Compostela

For the most pious travellers from Lorraine and Burgundy who left from Vézelay, Périgueux was the main stop over after Limoges. Located along the *via Lemovicensis*, along with the *via Tolosana,* the *via Podiensis* and the *via Turonensis,* one of the four most frequented paths taken by pilgrims during the Middle Ages on their way to Compostela, Périgueux was already mentioned during the 12th century in Aimery Picaud's Pilgrim's Guide. He recommended to the faithful that they come venerate Saint Front's relics, for his tomb, built like the Holy Sepulchre, was "more beautiful in its craftsmanship than all the other saints' tombs combined". Such a beautiful church could only be dedicated to a great saint... and yet, blessed Front's life remains quite obscure, even completely legendary. It seems the church of Périgueux wanted to enhance the story of its origins. They attributed an exceptional personality to their first bishop and spiced up his life with fantastic tales, for the most part borrowed from the lives of other saints, especially his immediate rival Saint Martial of Limoges. As the story goes, Front was allegedly consecrated bishop by Saint Peter himself and sent to evangelize Perigord at the beginning of Christianity. He was said to have performed many miracles: his prayer made a statue of Venus fall apart from which a dragon emerged, bringing down seven pagans; he resuscitated his companion with the help of a pastoral staff given to him by Saint Peter and was able to be in two places at once, attending Saint Martha's funeral in Tarascon in Provence while saying mass in Périgueux. Having also rid Perigord of a monstrous serpent by simply making the sign of the cross, Saint Front was often invoked for protection against reptiles.

do homes and businesses of merchants growing rich off this activity. Le Puy-Saint Front district grew in stature. There then sprang up a disagreeable rivalry between the old fortified town, teetering in the tatters of its former splendour, and the new borough, dynamic and bustling, with its sights set on business and the accumulation of wealth. It was at this point that the two enemy sisters, situated on the border of beautiful Guienne, bequeathed by Eleanor of Aquitaine to her legitimate children, the kings of England, had to take sides. Le Puy-Saint Front had French leanings and the old town failed to make its voice heard. Quite to the contrary, it saw itself sucked into a union that played right into the hands of its busy neighbour. In 1240, the two towns became the two districts of one and the same community, which took the name of Périgueux. Some of the town's most famous historical remains date from the Middle Ages. The church of Saint Étienne de la Cité was the first major Christian edifice in the old fortified quarter. It suffered severe damage during the Wars of Religion, but had been a huge cathedral, sober and elegant, with five bays covered by the rounded firmament of its five domes. All that remains of this splendid structure are the two east bays, where you can still make out the ancient wounds of the dismantled walls. This is one of the oldest domed churches in Perigord, and it is still a main source in any analysis of Romanesque art in the region. Le Puy-St.Front district, for centuries well protected behind its ramparts, has preserved its medieval look, and part of its medieval soul, too. The walls have gone, leaving just a few massive witnesses, like the 15th century Mataguerre tower, delimited by the elegant fringe of its machicolations. It is well worth venturing into the maze of small streets lined with picture-book façades: Gothic and pointed arches lowering over beautiful studded doors, polygonal towers clinging to the sharp corners of the buildings along the Rue des Farges, and the impressive mansions on Rue Aubergerie.

Périgueux: the Consul's Mansion

Rue Limogeanne, now a pedestrian precinct as it was in the Middle Ages, is lined with magnificent Renaissance mansions with carved pediments. On the banks of the Isle, several fine residences have been preserved, their roofs punctuated with intricately carved dormer windows, like those of the Consul's Mansion. A small wood-and-daub structure, perched high on a pedestal made of heavy stones, once surveyed the river, and, quite erroneously, bears the name: The Old Mill. It is in fact the old granary of the monks of the Saint Front chapter, and it has somehow managed to avoid both destruction by man and the perilous assaults of the river. In the heart of this medieval town stands Périgueux's most famous monument. Saint Front Cathedral, built in the 12th century on the site of the ancient tomb of the apostle of Perigord, is one of France's most extraordinary churches. Are we in Perigord or Byzantium? From the great basilicas of the east, it has borrowed its Greek cross layout with the branches strictly identical, and its

domes and cupolas. The array of pinnacle turrets with small regular peristyles, rising in a crescendo from the turrets at the chancel end to the pointed shape of the great bell-tower is the outcome of almost overly perfect restoration work carried out in the 19th century. The new bell-tower has preserved the style of the 12th century original, and rises up at the junction of the two parts forming the present-day edifice. The two 11th century bays crowned by lofty domes have not been greatly altered. The four large domes on pendentives are supported by colossal pillars carved in the form of a cross. A small chapel off the north transept still houses a special piece of furniture. Two front panels of carved wood depict Saint Front, on the left, slaying the legendary serpent of the tower of Vesona, and Saint Martha, on the right, trampling the *tarasque*, a mythical monster. All that remains of the monastery buildings is a magnificent cloister, with its handsome central structure in the form of a pine-cone, which once sat on top of the bell-tower.

Périgueux, Saint Front Cathedral: St. Front slaying the serpent and St. Martha trampling the tarasque

The Perigord Museum of Art and Archaeology

L ocated on the Cours Tourny since 1869, in buildings built specially between 1895 and 1898 on the site of the city's former Augustine convent, the Museum of Archaeology, Fine Arts and Primary Arts of Périgueux protects and preserves vast collections. There are about 45.000 pieces, of which about 10% are on display. Mainly coming from the treasures accumulated by the region in the course of its long history, these collections also consist of works and objects from other parts of Europe, Africa, Oceania, America and Asia – the generous donations of local collectors. The prehistory department possesses not only an important set of flint tools, but also fossilized remains of our ancestors: the skeleton of Régourdou Man (Neanderthal), intentionally buried 70.000 years ago, and that of Chancelade Man (*Homo sapiens*), buried in a foetal position during the Magdalenian period (18.000 to 11.000 B.C.) The painted blocks in the Blanchard Shelter (dated to 35.000 years ago), the admirable, finely carved objects in

Mosaic known as *Flora's Head*, 2nd c. or early 3rd c., from La Boissière d'Ans

Engraved disc, Magdalenian period, from La Laugerie Basse

bone or flint from the Magdalenian period, like the bison pendant, but also the painted pebbles from Mas d'Azil, all moving testimony of these first humans who were already in search of Beauty, posed questions about death and apparently had precise religious rituals. The Gallo-Roman collections – remarkable mosaics, frescoes, statuettes or architectural elements – evoke the entire territory of the Petrocorii's *civitas*, which corresponded more or less to the area of the current department of Dordogne. The medieval collection contains fine remnants – capitals, 12th century metopes, a 13th century reredos – from the former church of Saint Front. A rare piece, the Rabastens diptych, painted on parchment at the end of the 13th century, illustrates the Passion of Christ and the Dormition of the Virgin. In the Renaissance collections, the visitor should note the fine ivory sculpture of Saint Michael overcoming the dragon, and, in a completely different style, a painting attributed to Peter Huys (†1584), showing the extraction of the Stone of Madness. The museum also displays some remarkable paintings from the 17th, 18th and 19th centuries. It is hence a veritable journey through the ages, through time and civilization that is proposed by the Museum of Perigord. It also has an entire series of masks and statues from indigenous societies in Africa and Oceania, objects that were principally collected by prehistorians. The Asian section contains, among other things, fine porcelains, and the American collections include pieces ranging from Inuit figures with strange, ghostly shapes to necklaces made by the Galibi Indians of Guyane, objects linked to shamanic practices.

The Stone of Madness, attributed to Peter Huys, oil on wood panel

Pierre de Bourdeille, School of Clouet, 16th century, oil on canvas

Pendant with bison, Magdalenian, from the Raymonden Shelter

Chancelade and Merlande

A few miles from Périgueux, hidden in the wooded Beauronne valley, stands Chancelade Abbey. Founded in the 12th century, close to a spring, Chancelade, the latticed fountain (from the Latin *fons cancellatus*), swiftly became an important abbey. The monks there chose the Augustinian rule to organize their community. During the Hundred Years' War English troops set up camp here and put the monks to flight. A long period of decline set in, worsened still further by the merciless struggle that pitted Catholics and Protestants in the 16th century. The abbey had to wait patiently until the 17th century, before it could once more enjoy a state of calm. Worn and polished to a sheen, the large round flagstones of the main entrance lead as if naturally to a verdant area. A 12th century inscription reminds us that the founding hermit went by the name of Folcaudus or Foucault. The buildings form an almost perfect quadrilateral around the central courtyard. They house a flat-vaulted vat-house where the monks used to make their wine, and even distilled the alcohol required by their infirmary. The stables, which have sadly lost their magnificent timber-work, still present a fine aspect. Adjoining them are the monks' workshops built as a series of small, low rooms surmounted by a handsome stone balustrade. The heavy, fortified mill, complete with a draw-bridge, surveys an arm of the river Beauronne. Above the murmuring water, the gardens offer a profusion of rustling hydrangea blooms at the foot of the old walls. The main so-called Bourdeille building, with its very severe outer façade, presents on the garden side, all the refinement of 15th century edifices. Two turrets flank a sharp-pointed gable decorated with *fleurs-de-lys* and kale motifs. A grand door with fine sculptures opens on to a spiral staircase. Much of the cloister has disappeared, but the truncated stumps of the columns that still survive form a setting that is as romantic as you could wish. At the far end of the gardens, the so-called Abbot's lodge is a huge residence which opens on to a vaulted gallery, with a balustered terrace running alongside it. The dormer windows are decorated with pediments sculpted with the arms of the abbey. The Romanesque abbey church has a beautiful arcaded façade and a corbelled cornice. The doorway is bounded by arch mouldings underscored by the fine, regular line of their 'nail-head' sculptures. A three-storey bell-tower rises up above the crossing of the nave and transept, itself topped by a cupola on pendentives. The choir is decorated with 14th century frescoes. Beside Saint Christopher, those medieval artists would also have been keen to depict Saint Thomas à Becket, the archbishop of Canterbury murdered in 1170, for whom these monks showed a special devotion. The chapel of Saint John, close by, is one of those tiny, charming buildings, that only Romanesque art was capable of creating. Close to the abbey, at the foot of a crag, Raymonden Cave housed prehistoric treasures, including the burial place of the famous "Chancelade man", a Magdalenian.

Geoffroy de Cauze, the bishop of Périgueux, joined Merlande Priory to Chancelade Abbey in 1140. Despite its being hidden away in the forest of Feytaud, it suffered from the same tragic events as its mother abbey. The main part of the priory dates from the 12th century. Huge vaults and a dome on pendentives soar above the nave and lead toward the choir, reached through a triumphal pointed arch resting on capitals carved with lions. In the choir, the original chapel, eleven other sculpted capitals present lions or wild animals among vegetation. There is a striking contrast between the cold sobriety of the nave and the exuberance of these capitals. The church had been provided with strong-rooms in the extrados of the vaults in the choir, the dome and the nave. During the 16th century, another room was arranged at the top of the building's north-east corner.

Around Périgueux

The castle of Château-l'Évêque, which used to belong to the bishops of Périgueux, stands on the shores of the Beauronne River. Most of it was built in the 14th century, but it underwent transformation in the 15th and 16th centuries. It was in the castle's oratory that Vincent de Paul celebrated his first mass in 1600.

The Romanesque church of Saint Martin of Agonac, also on the Beauronne's shores, was built in the 11th and 12th centuries. Its bell-tower is topped by a defensive chamber. The building, with its strict right angles, consists of parallel blocks fitted together. The whole gives an impression of great severity, tempered only by the ochre-russet colours of its stone and its funerary niches.

With its two round, white towers crowned with smooth, symmetrical roofs, Bories Castle, near Antonne-et-Trigonant in the Isle River valley, was built from 1497 to 1602, hence the evident Renaissance influences. It was besieged four times during the Wars of Religion and the Fronde, but suffered little damage. The main building is flanked by a large, square keep facing the river through its staggered row of mullioned windows. A balustrade with columns overlooks the river Isle. In the basement, a kitchen with ribbed vaulting supported by strong pillars has been restored. Two huge fireplaces are embellished with a magnificent mantelpiece in the form of a very flat arch resting on two small brick pillars.

South-east of Périgueux, the Gothic church at La Douze was built during the 14th and 15th centuries. Its Renaissance-style furnishing is exceptional in Perigord. The three panels in the pulpit, within frames trimmed with plant motifs, depict the arms of the Baron de la Douze, Pierre d'Abzac, and his wife, Jeanne de Bourdeille. Saint Peter stands between them, in the centre. The reredos is decorated with statues of the married pair captured in the humble posture of prayer and meditation.

The fortress of Grignols is an imposing ruin situated high above the Vern River valley. The castle, which used to control the road between Périgueux and Bordeaux, was besieged several times and was demolished during the Fronde in 1652. The keep, with its rows of smooth stones, is crowned with a row of merlons. The parapet walk and the curtain walls that have resisted destruction also display the well-defined lines of their merlons, like embroidery on the battlements. All that remains of this huge construction with its tangled and partly-demolished rooms are the enormous walls where fine fireplaces with intricate sculptures can be seen.

Saint Astier is a small town in the Isle valley, with its houses clustered around a church whose mighty belfry is supported by four corner buttresses. Its shallow-pitched roof is topped by a central pinnacle. Fine Renaissance houses with orange-hued roofs descend in rows to the edge of the waters of the Isle, streaming over a causeway covered with white froth.

Sorges, the House of Truffles

The town of Sorges honours the mushroom which softened the blow struck by phylloxera, by growing in the abandoned vineyards. All the secrets of the 'black diamond' are revealed, from its formation to its harvest, from its storage to its culinary uses. A path running through truffle-rich ground allows the visitor to discover the conditions required for the production of the *tuber melanosporum*, better known as the Perigord truffle. Hidden away in the chalky earth, it grows at the foot of hazel or oak tree; the tree provides carbon matter to the mushroom, which provides, which minerals to the tree. Once winter has arrived, it reachs full maturity. Tracked down by the keen sense of smell of a sow or a dog, or betrayed by a cloud of flies, the truffle is found and finally ready to offer up its subtle flavour.

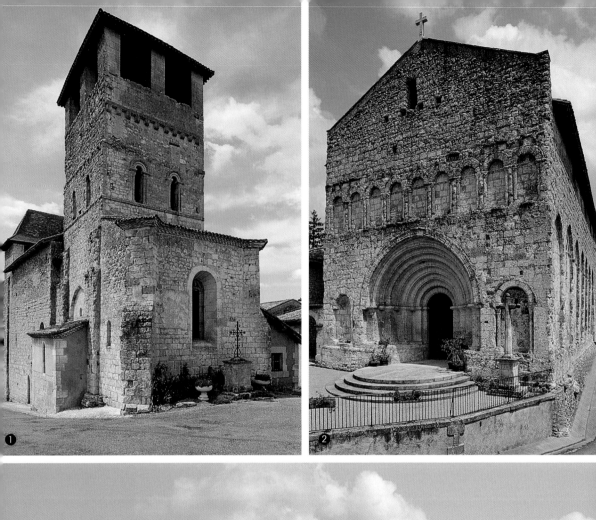

6

WHITE AND GREEN PERIGORDS

The Ribéracois

The Ribéracois, or White Perigord, is particularly rich in Romanesque domed churches. Saint Pierre-ès-Liens-Church in Siorac-de-Ribérac reaches skyward, its tall steeple capping a tiny nave. A dome tops the chancel, as in Notre Dame Church in Vanxains. Near Vanxains, well hidden from visitors in the heart of the forest, stands the natural line of large stones at Sauteranne. The moss-covered boulders have taken on natural hues, the better to blend in with their surroundings.

Saint Privat-des-Prés Church, the former priory of a Benedictine establishment, was built in the 12th century. It is mentioned in 1180, in the cartulary of La Sauve-Majeure Abbey. From the doorway with its semi-circular vaulting, nine voussoirs form perfect concentric lines, lending the austere façade a recessed relief, delimited by a final archivolt in the form of a regular frieze. Two small barrel-vaulted archways symmetrically reproduce the gentle curve of the Romanesque arches. The doorway is surmounted by nine blind arches resting on slender triple-shafted columns. Evidence of its role as a fortress can be seen in the defensive passages, merlons, crenellations, and the fortified belfry. Inside, the central nave with its pointed barrel vaulting is shaped like an irregular rectangle, and the two side aisles are slightly sloped. The transept crossing is vaulted with a dome; the apse is a semi-dome vault.

The fully fortified church of Saints Peter and Paul in Grand Brassac is extremely sober, but its north façade is adorned with fine sculptures representing the Lamb and the evangelists surrounding Christ. Three

Domed Churches

The Ribéracois presents an exceptional number of the domed churches that are considered as the original expression of Perigourdian Romanesque art. The origin of these vaults remains uncertain; local for some, they result from the rounded roofs of shepherds' huts; Oriental for others, they are an adaptation of Byzantine architecture discovered and brought back by pilgrims and crusaders from the time of the Crusades. Whatever the explication, the dome turned out to be the best solution to the vault problems of Romanesque master builders since the barrel vault in use required a complicated buttressing mechanism. The dome, in comparison, provided an even distribution of the thrust on the lateral walls, as well as the transverse ribs of the nave. Moreover, it seems that solidity of construction was a priority since these churches also served in the villages' defense. Few sculpted adornments decorate the capitals of the columns and the portal, the inner space is very opened up and the extreme simplicity of line leaves everything to the spare beauty of the limestone masonry. However reminiscent of the east these domed churches may be, the Ribéracois churches are never built to the Greek cross plan. A succession of three or four domes top the nave and form a whole with the line leading from the entrance to the apse. A bell tower, often fortified, completes the whole, while many later alterations serve as a reminder of the vissicitudes of history.

domes on pendentives top its narrow, raised nave.

The nave of the church in Cherval has four domes. The one over the choir is encircled by a frieze sculpted in nailhead motifs. Nearby, La Tour Blanche Castle stands on a feudal hillock. A possession of the Counts of Angoulême, it passed to the Bourdeille. Brantôme used to visit his grandmother there. A keep is extended by a main building flanked by a narrow tower fortified with a stone hoarding.

The village of Paussac also has a domed church. Paussac dolmen, called Peyrelevade or standing stone, is one of many traces left in Perigord by Neolithic Man.

Upstream from Bourdeilles, in the Dronne River valley, the rock called the Devil's Furnace, containing prehistoric deposits from the Solutrean era, is famous for the stone block carved with cattle, which is now on display at the Prehistory Museum in Les Eyzies.

Devil's Furnace Rock

Cherval: Saint Martin's Church

Bourdeilles

Bourdeilles castle is one of the four grand castles proudly bearing the title of barony of Perigord. On its rocky promontory overlooking the river Dronne, Bourdeilles is not what it first appears, for it is not one castle, but a brace.

The medieval edifice, built from the 13th to the 15th century, is an austere building whose main function was to protect those taking refuge within it. A completely paved courtyard, bounded by tall crenellated curtain walls, leads to a main building where one thrusting corner seems poised over the Dronne flowing far below. The huge polygonal keep rising up above the ramparts lends Bourdeilles the look of a fortress, bristling with machicolations. It was here that Philip the Fair locked many a Templar away in the dungeons. The Renaissance castle is really a small square palace, where elegance and refinement vie with the sumptuousness of the decoration and furnishings. It was the creation of, and designed by, Jacquette de Montbron, wife of André de Bourdeille, who was keen to dazzle her sovereign, Catherine de' Medici. The great 16th century fireplace on the first floor is evidence of a most confident taste, typical of these eminently wealthy and influential people. All the furnishings (be it the canopied beds and armchairs, or the woodwork, tapestries and tiling) go to make this castle a wonder to behold, even today. The attention to detail extended even to the design of the raised flower-beds at the foot of the castle walls, and a lawn shaped like a fleur-de-lis. The river Dronne laps against the tall, moss-covered walls, and reflects the pale stonework of this jewel in its deep blue waters. Set on its prow-like stone perch, a small mill bravely cleaves the tumbling current of the river.

And to complete the picture, the gentle arch of a Gothic bridge spans the mirror formed by the momentarily still waters.

Bourdeilles, the Renaissance Castle: the Golden Salon

Brantôme

Located on the shores of a meander of the Dronne River, Brantôme is one of the most attractive sites in this area of Perigord. During the High Middle Ages, a small community of hermits settled at the foot of the cliff, where water surged out of the rock. They lived in the caves that were naturally gouged out of the cliff-face. In 769, Charlemagne founded the abbey of Brantôme and entrusted it with the relics of Saint Sicaire, one of the Holy Innocents. The Benedictine monks of Brantôme decided to take advantage of the gift provided by Nature and built their abbey with stones quarried from the cliff. They did not, however, abandon the troglodytic rooms, but installed their heating room, washing place, a mill and a dovecote in them. They even took refuge there when the Norsemen looted and destroyed their abbey during the 9th century. It was rebuilt by Abbot William in the 11th century. In the

Dreams and Miniatures

Born of Madame du Parc Locmaria's passion for doll furniture, the *Musée Rêve et Miniature*, the Dreams and Miniatures Museum, first opened its doors in 1996, inviting the public into the private world of the home seen from the inside. Six houses built on a doll's scale allow the discovery of the world of interior decoration as much in the evolution of styles, from the Middle Ages to today, as in techniques of manufacturing. A child's imagination is not forgotten, for there are funny little houses to be discovered, inhabited by animals such as mice and beetles. Built on a scale of 1/12th, the furniture and decors are identical to their life-sized versions, from the smallest details in a key-hole and marquetry to that pair of glasses, forgotten on a sofa, which give a living spirit to these miniature homes.

Brantôme, the cave dovecote: the calvary

The kitchen of La Jauneraye Manor

16th, the abbey came under the commendam system, with its abbot chosen from among members of the secular clergy. Pierre de Mareuil and his nephew, Pierre de Bourdeille, were both commendatory abbots. The abbey church has been much restored since its original construction in the 11th century. Only the 35 metre-high steeple dates from that period. Standing away from the church, its five-storied structure extends the rocky spur on which it stands. The domes of the nave have disappeared and been replaced by Angevin-style vaulting. The convent buildings and the cloister have also been transformed. Today, they contain the town hall offices and the collections of the Fernand-Desmoulin Museum. During the 15th century, in one of the troglodytic rooms, called the Cave of the Final Judgement, the monks had a Triumph of Death sculpted. The sculptures blend into a rather obscure and symbolic stone blur. On the right side, a calvary with carved figures shows a later, more conventional style.

To take full advantage of Brantôme's location, the visitor should venture away from the cliff and cross the pretty angled bridge that spans the Dronne. The water has been tamed and channelled, murmuring over a weir fringed with froth, nonchalantly turning an ancient moss-covered paddle-wheel, glistening with the sparkle of its rivulets. The old houses, well-preserved in their fleece of dark green ivy, are reflected, not without a dash of vanity, in the calm waters of the Dronne.

Between 1550 and 1580 Pierre de Bourdeille had Richemont Castle built several leagues north of Brantôme Abbey, of which he was the commendatory abbot. At his death in 1614, he was buried in the chapel he had had built in 1610, and whose inscription he wrote. He was very attached to this residence, which had cost him no less than 20.000 ecus, and wrote, "My house is beautiful Castle of Richemont that I had built curiously and with difficulty and great cost where the air is fine, good and healthy".

Bourdeille or Brantôme?

A curious character with two names so closely linked that they leave you with the disquieting impression that you have somewhere gone astray in the complex genealogy of this family. His real name is Pierre de Bourdeille, born in 1540, third scion and thus barred from the title of the renowned Bourdeille family by an all-powerful law of primogeniture. But the monarchs were not unsympathetic to the plight of these younger sons. So we find him nominated abbot of Brantôme, whence the other surname... It goes without saying that he professed the faith, but did he really have the calling? He travelled widely and spent most of his life in the army and at royal courts, for he saw in three kings, François II, Charles IX and Henry III, and became the faithful friend of the regent, Catherine de' Medici. Steering clear of the fierce rivalries that pitted Catholic against Protestant, this consummate diplomat skillfully exercised his art to the utmost to prevent his abbey from being laid waste by fire and bloodshed. But he also enjoyed writing, and showed a spirited style well able to entrance many a reader curious enough to delve into his *Chronicles*, *Lives of Illustrious Men and Great Captains* and *Lives of Gallant Ladies*. A few miles from his abbey, our brave Brantôme, or rather Pierre de Bourdeille, had Richemont castle built on top of a well-exposed rise. This stark, almost austere castle has a lean look beneath its huge roof. In compliance with his wishes, Brantôme was buried in the crypt of the castle's funerary chapel.

The chapel's very Baroque decoration was intended to call to mind the inevitable outcome of life, and it was his decision to adorn the walls with macabre friezes.

From Mareuil to Nontron

Mareuil is one of the four baronies that ruled Perigord for several centuries. Its 15th century castle is now reduced to the striking ruins of a fortress, showing an extremely advanced system of fortifications. There is no handy inaccessible rock pinnacle or sheer cliff here. Instead, corner towers, round and square alike, were added, and all access ways reinforced.

Beyond the first gatehouse, built like a fortified barbican, a narrow and well guarded flight of steps leads to the drawbridge and its entrance gate flanked by two huge round towers, crowned by watch-paths and machicolations. The small chapel squeezed inside the building is a marvel in the Flamboyant Gothic style. The vault with hanging keystones is entirely ribbed with fine, festooned arches. The square structure of the main building, with beautiful mullioned windows, contains Renaissance elements. The troubadour Arnaud lived at Mareuil castle in the 12th century. In the pure tradition of courtly love, he has left us his tender songs inspired by his chatelaine, Adelaide, wife of the viscount of Beziers. But Mareuil is also the name of those valiant warrior barons proudly accompanying the king of France at Bouvines in 1214, or, later in 1370, taking part in Du Guesclin's expedition to liberate Perigord.

Renowned for its knife manufacturing, Nontron is located in the heart of a beautiful region full of interesting, not always well-known sites. To the northwest, the Saint Robert Chapel is Romanesque. At Teyjat, a small cave conceals some very refined and interesting rock engravings, the work of the last Magdalenians. The Nontronneau excavations, nearby, have unearthed an important Gallo-Roman site. "Tottering Rock", a huge, precariously poised granite boulder, lies near Saint Estephe pond. And to the east, the Dronne cascades over rocks at the Chalard waterfall.

The Tottering Rock near Saint-Estèphe

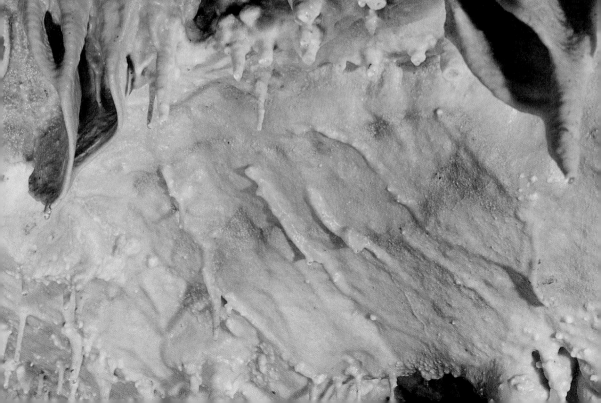

Villars

The maze-like network of Villars cave emerges on to the wooded slopes of the picturesque Trincou valley. At the end of a long, narrow corridor, the chambers open out on to a fairy-tale setting. The most recent stalactites colonize the roofs with their myriad needle-sharp points. The cleverly choreographed lighting enacts a ballet of reflections and colour-tones which forge volumes out of unreal shapes. Like some sumptuous fabric, an amazing mineral hanging has been tossed casually over the edge of an overhang. Beneath our very eyes, the slow metamorphosis worked by time and water throws the very structure of the rock into a state of apparent motionlessness. The rounded flows of calcite swell noiselessly with thousands of quietly sparkling particles.

Prehistoric people, undoubtedly among the earliest Magdalenian groupings, ventured into the bowels of the earth and left behind the strange vestiges of the things that concerned them. An exceptional mural of horses looms gradually beneath the calcite flows which thicken and lend these drawings an amazing bluish hue. A small blue horse darts off without a sound, its slender legs outstretched in a wild gallop. The confidence of the stroke and the rendering of the movement turn this simple sketch into a masterpiece. But the most striking of all the Villars depictions is still the diminutive man, almost grotesquely contorted, arms raised, legs braced, confronting a bison putting the whole weight of its wrath behind its charge. This is a strange and rare scene indeed, pitting man against beast face-to-face, just as in the Well Gallery at Lascaux. These treasures are not the only ones present in the cave. The layer of translucent calcite, which confirms their authenticity, has turned into an opaque carapace, doubtless burying some figures that once decorated this sanctuary cave. A local Prehistory Museum is being set up.

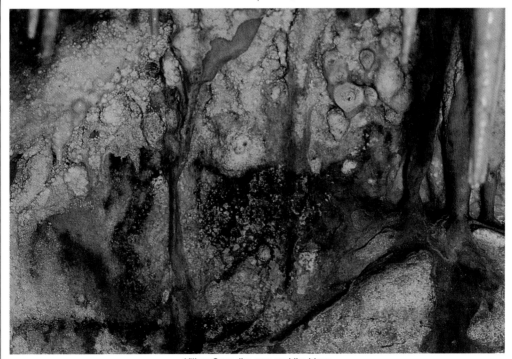

Villars Cave: the man and the bison

Puyguilhem

Located near the village of Villars, in a pastoral valley, Puyguilhem is a magnificent Renaissance mansion similar to the great castles in the Loire River valley. It was certainly built in the early 16th century by Mondot de La Marthonie, President of the Parliament of Bordeaux, then of Paris. Mondot de La Marthonie was chosen by King François I as administrator of the Kingdom of France during the royal expedition to Italy. But this supreme honour kept him away from his Perigord castle, and he died in Blois in 1517.

Fine round or pentagonal towers, a monumental fireplace decorated with the Twelve Labours of Hercules in the great hall on the first floor, walnut-wood timber work on the second floor, a profusion of dormer windows and chimneys sprouting from the long, even-tiled roofs, windows adorned with panels sculpted with intricate traceries of dovetailed lettering, made even more intricate by the mixture of supple lines of ropes, chains and crowns – all attest to the wealth and taste of the Marthonies.

Beneath the roof of the polygonal tower, inside which climbs a spiral staircase, a procession of rather esoteric letters decorate a cornice. They might be an allusion to the architect who designed the castle. A bas-relief on the door of the south-west tower is carved with the initials of Mondot de La Marthonie and his wife, Anna de Vernon. The main staircase, beneath its coffered ceiling, leads to the rooms of the main dwelling which contain several Aubuisson tapestries and fine carved chests. Today the property of the Dordogne department, Puyguilhem Castle holds regular exhibitions in its prestigious surroundings.

Barely two kilometres away, west of Puyguilhem, stand the ruins of the Cistercian Abbey of Boschaud.

Puyguilhem Castle: the monumental fireplace decorated with the Six Labours of Hercules

Boschaud Abbey

This ancient abbey belonging to the Cistercian order was founded in the 12th century in the depths of a small wooded valley. Boschaud suffered sorely from the brutality of the Hundred Years' War, and not much less from the Wars of Religion. Boschaud Abbey now stands in ruins, but the beauty of the remains of this arresting building are well worth a detour. Swathed in woodland, the slender, white silhouette of the abbey offers up to the sky the elegant remnants of a dome, now frail and teetering. What refinement, despite that Cistercian commitment to simplicity! The sweeping grasslands that lap at the foot of the long walls shed a gentle light over the soft blond stones. Majestic walnut trees cool the tops of the walls with their delicate shadows. There is total hush here, and silence shrouds the secrets of this valley in mysterious peace and quiet.

Boschaud Abbey

Boschaud Abbey

Saint-Jean-de-Côle

The small, fortified medieval village of Saint-Jean-de-Côle developed around an 11th century Augustinian priory. The serenity emanating from its serried houses, protecting one another for mutual safety, is perfectly at one with the tranquillity of the dark woodland surrounding it. The river Côle flows over a bed of pebbles, crossed by a ford. An old humpbacked Gothic bridge covered with smooth cobblestones reflects its small round arches in the river's calm waters. La Marthonie Castle, elegantly silhouetted above the village square, was built in the early 14th century and was completed with a Renaissance wing in the 17th century.

The Church of Saint John the Baptist is the former priory. Built in the mid-12th century, it has resisted the trials endured by the prior and his canons: English occupation at the end of the 14th century, followed by Protestants in the 16th century. Original in form, it has a rounded single nave and the apse opens onto two small radiating chapels. The large dome that once covered the nave collapsed more than once and has not been rebuilt. Its square 17th century belfry, pierced with openings, watches over the building. Inside the church, a Virgin with Child is a charming, 16th century bas-relief, and a recess in the south chapel contains a damaged recumbent figure of a prior. The exterior capitals of the chevet are carved with scenes popular with medieval artists such as Daniel in the Lions' Den or the drunken Noah. The modillions supporting the roof of the apse and the apsidal chapels are carved with masks, wrestlers, contortionists and other legendary animals. A small covered market leans up against one of the apsidal chapels. Behind the church, vestiges of the priory's cloister are still visible.

The wrath of sky and man

Lightning struck and devastated the 15th-17th century castle of La Chapelle-Faucher, with its fine, regular façade, lent further symmetry by two well-proportioned dormer windows surmounted by ridge ornaments, two pepper-pot turrets, and two large recessed towers. The crenellated outlines of its parapet walk now look down upon an empty building where the fire caused by the bolt merrily consumed the wealth of ages accumulated within its walls. But its lofty rooms have often been dogged by high drama, because before the fire there was bloodshed. According to Brantôme, chronicler of the Wars of Religion, the castle was the scene of a terrible event. Close to 260 Catholic peasants were slaughtered in the lower hall of the castle by the troops of Admiral de Coligny, on July 2, 1569. But the castle still bears itself proudly on its rock, dominating the small Côle valley in all its splendour.

La Chapelle-Faucher Castle

Excideuil and Tourtoirac

Excideuil Castle stands on top of a sheer cliff. Two square keeps linked by a curtain wall date from the 12th and 13th centuries. This medieval part of the fortress was besieged several times, including by Richard the Lionheart. An adjacent main building with a turret was altered during the 16th century. Only the church, radically altered during the 15th century, remains of Excideuil's old, 12th century Benedictine priory.

Vestiges of the Benedictine abbey of Tourtoirac are scattered around the presbytery gardens. The abbey church originally had a clover-leaf layout, but only the 12th century transept still stands. Under the vault of the Romanesque chapel, *echea* – rounded, embedded pieces of pottery – improved the acoustics. One of the capitals in the chapter house is carved with monks mischievously pulling on each others' beards.

King of Patagonia!

Born in Perigord in 1825, Antoine de Tounens was a lawyer in Périgueux, but it was not his lot to end his days in a stuffy office. He would be king! So he had to choose a kingdom, and in that day and age thrones were not two-a-penny. Undeterred, he looked further afield, to South America, symbol of fortunes to be made for the asking. He borrowed money and next thing we find him dashing between Chile and Argentina, to carve himself a kingdom in the sun. In 1860, he was named King of Arauconia, crowned by a tribe of indios, with the most royal name of Orélie-Antoine I. His Chilean neighbours had him arrested and deported. Nine years later he tried all over again. This second deportation was for good, and his wild dreams were shattered. He died in Tourtoirac in 1878.

Excideuil: the castle

Hautefort

A castle of elegance and harmony, like a phoenix risen from the ashes! On the night of 30-31 August 1968, a terrible fire ravaged the place, and people were sure it had joined the long list of imposing ruins. The main building was completely destroyed by the blaze, and the terrifying photos taken that night still bear witness to the scale of the disaster. With brave determination, Baron de Bastard, owner of the castle, aided by the Historic Monuments board and the considerable proceeds of a national subscription, managed to rebuild the damaged building. Hautefort has indeed recovered its former glory. Needless to say, in the rooms, the furniture devoured by the flames has been impossible to replace, and the whole north wing is out of bounds to visitors.

The troubadour Bertran de Born was lord of Hautefort. He was at his most poetic when he sang the praises of his lady in such courtly terms: "My lady is radiant and fair, loveable and young, her skin as white as hawthorn...". But he was also a fearsome warrior who "...would happily break lances, pierce shields and bucklers, cleave gleaming helmets, and deliver mighty blows..." With gallant self-confidence he played a busy part in the vagaries of a feudal history where might and cunning went hand in glove. Bertran de Born's heirs bore the name of Hautefort to the peak of its glory, when, in 1614, King Louis XIII made the fief a marquisate.

A few years later, this same Louis would succumb, hook, line and sinker, to the charms of the virtuous and beautiful Marie de Hautefort, sister of the marquis, Jacques François de Hautefort, who had his stronghold transformed into a palatial Renaissance castle with the help of the architect Nicolas Rambourg. The esplanade that leads up to the castle looks down on the deep cutting used by the road, and takes you straight to a narrow drawbridge flanked by two pepper-pot turrets.

Hautefort Castle: the courtyard

Hautefort is an imposing four-sided structure, consisting, on the north side, of a main Renaissance-style building, with large regular windows and two perpendicular wings adjoined at the end by two large round towers, crowned by a dome-shaped roof and an elegant pinnacle turret. Some of the rooms have preserved their original furniture and beautiful 16th and 17th century Flemish tapestries. The staircase, entirely restored, and identical to the original, is majestic, and the small chapel, miraculously saved from the fire, is a delightful 17th century building, comfortably housed in the large south-east tower.

It is well worth climbing to the top of the south-west tower to get an idea of what the old timber-work of the castle used to be like. An elegant frame, built entirely of chestnut, extends into a lofty, rounded cupola covered with attractive slates above the old parapet walk that once crowned the tower.

Hautefort castle is very Loire-like in its architecture, and very Versailles-like in its gardens. The arabesques, stars, crosses, and arcs, all pruned with compass and ruler amid the tamed greenery, are something to feast the eyes upon. The spotless walks underscore the regular and symmetrical velvet of the higher ground, and even the trees are arrayed in serried ranks on the steep slope of the rocky crag on which the castle sits perched.

An amazing tunnel has been cut among the dense branches of a double row of fragrant yew trees. Nothing remains of the classic shape of these shrubs, now pruned, trained and snipped until they agree to grow in the perfect casting of a dome-shaped rotunda, and a long open pergola with small square windows. The gardens and parklands of Hautefort are superb and cover more than 100 acres, rising to the top of the gently rounded mound of the furthest hill. Paths and walks make for pleasing strolls beneath venerable old trees.

To the east, the present parish church used to be a 17th century hospice, built to a Greek cross design around a circular chapel.

Hautefort Castle: timber-work in the south-west tower

The castle and the forge at Savignac-Lédrier

Inside the forge

In the 15th century, the forge-masters, the Pasquet de Savignac family, had their castle built north-east of Hautefort. From its windows they could survey the forge located at the foot of its walls. In 1656, the castle and forge became the property of the Lubersac family. For many a century, men had been aware of the advantages to be derived from the many waterfalls which check the flow of small torrents and streams tumbling rowdily down the outermost spurs of the Massif Central. There were consequently lots of forges in Perigord, and many of them continued their activity until the Second Empire (the period from 1852-1871, under Napoleon III).The forges at Savignac-Lédrier are not unlike a long-surviving fossil, since they began to work in 1421 and were put back into activity by the Combescot family during the 19th century. All the ingredients

The castle and the forge

required were at hand and available to the peasant labourers: ore in the topmost layers of the soil, rich woodlands supplying an apparently inexhaustible source of fuel for making charcoal and above all, the power of water to drive the ingenious machinery capable of crushing, grinding and pulverizing. Smelting furnaces were even installed at Savignac-Lédrier. The last evidence of this bygone metalworking is the knives of Nontron, with their painstakingly worked box-wood handles. The decline of the charcoal-fuelled forges was nevertheless irrevocable, and Green Perigord is now trying to make a last bid to exploit the resources of its valleys by exhibiting this time-honoured activity as part of a display of "industrial archaeology". As for the castle, it was transformed or enlarged several times over the course of the 16th, 17th and 19th centuries. In the park still stands a Renaissance gateway, a symbol of the wealth and power of the forge-masters.

Jumilhac-le-Grand

In its present aspect, Jumilhac Castle dates only from the 16th and 17th centuries. A fortress stood on this site in the 13th century, but a master blacksmith, one Antoine Chapelle, enriched by the manufacture of iron in the nearby Isle valley, took for his wife the young lady of Jumilhac in 1579, and had a castle rebuilt, worthy of any recent aspirant to the nobility. Its extraordinary roof makes it one of the most eye-catching of all the great castles in Perigord. A spiral staircase gives access to a round, soothing room, haunted by the mystery of the "little Spinner". The south wing includes a fine main lodge built around a stone stairway leading to the panelled drawing-room, with a splendid inlaid parquet floor and a fireplace flanked by sculptures modelled in the round. Next door, Saint Pierre-ès-Liens church is Romanesque, but its choir was replaced by gothic-vaulted aisles in the 14th century.

And Louise spun…

The story has it that Louise, lovely Countess of Jumilhac, was shut away here, with distaff and spindles, by her jealous and suspicious husband. Beset by languor and boredom, Louise spun and spun all day long. But her kindly accomplice, the spindle, contained within it the tender messages that she secretly dispatched to the belovèd at the castle, who, in her ladyship's beautiful eyes, had become her simple shepherd. What has been handed down is a portrait of a young woman, her waist squeezed into a becoming, dark-hued bodice, plunging its point into a skirt with a huge apron trimmed with lace. A small coif covers the beautiful lady's tresses. In her left hand she holds a distaff, and absent-mindedly dangles a small spindle from her right hand.

Jumilhac-le-Grand Castle: the spinner's bedroom

INDEX